THE ART OF
A CAPPELLA SINGING

THE ART OF
A CAPPELLA SINGING

WITH SIXTEEN
REPRESENTATIVE WORKS

Containing instruction for singers in choral groups, to
promote an artistic ensemble; and analysis of the compositions
for technique, interpretation, and appreciation

By

JOHN SMALLMAN

Conductor of the *Smallman A Cappella Choir*, the *Los Angeles Oratorio Society*,
the *Cecilian Singers*, the *Woman's Choral Club of Pasadena*, and formerly Conductor
of various choirs in Boston, Massachusetts, and Southern California

AND

E. H. WILCOX

Formerly Professor of Music at the University of North Dakota,
the State University of Iowa, and Guest Professor at the University of
California at Berkeley and the University of Utah

2.00

OLIVER DITSON COMPANY
THEODORE PRESSER CO., DISTRIBUTORS
1712 CHESTNUT STREET
+ PHILADELPHIA +

Made in U. S. A.

FOREWORD

This book will assist in solving the problems of the individual voice, choral technique, repertoire, and interpretation.

I. THE INDIVIDUAL VOICE

Attention is given to the general principles of singing applicable to all types of voices and to all singers. Stress is placed on the necessity for free and adequate breathing, the tone sustaining qualities of vowel sounds, the expressive function of distinctly enunciated consonants, and the problem of accurate intonation.

Particular attention is given to pronunciation. Vocal sounds are classified in relation to four basic vocal positions. This is the simplest and most practical classification when dealing with large groups. Teachers who prefer to use a more elaborate vowel classification and procedure, or wish to change the order in which the vowel sounds are introduced, will find that this book adapts itself readily to such plans. Phonetic spelling, bringing out the sound characteristics of each word, is printed with all the music.

II. CHORAL TECHNIQUE

There are suggestions for the rehearsal room, the method of organizing the rehearsal period, the preliminary breathing and vocal exercises, and the problems of choral singing. A few of the more prominent choral problems discussed are intonation, blend, pronunciation, scale passages, chord balance, accent, phrase shape, rhythmic variety, form, expression, and interpretation.

III. REPERTOIRE

Sixteen notable pieces are included. Each one has musical merit of a high order.

Some of these are well known, others are heard only occasionally and a few are entirely new in a usable form.

Several are extremely simple, a few are fairly difficult, and there are all gradations between these extremes.

There is great variety of type. Secular numbers are chosen from French, German, Italian and English sources and the texts are adapted to present-day standards. Sacred numbers are selected from the Greek Orthodox, Roman Catholic and Protestant services. The list includes music for all occasions: sacred, secular, serious or gay.

All of the numbers can be sung without instrumental accompaniment although a piano reduction to two staves is printed.

The vocal range is practicable for the amateur choir. The tenor does not go above *F*, except in four pieces. In several pieces the bass does not go below *B♭* and it never goes below *G*. The lower limit for the alto is *A* except in two cases, but in five pieces *C* is the lower limit. The highest note for the soprano is *G*.

IV. INTERPRETATION

Marks of tempo, dynamics, and phrasing are unusually complete. The printed suggestions are extensive. Phonetic spelling, as an aid to accurate pronunciation, is given throughout.

This set of sixteen pieces is an introduction to standard choral literature of various nationalities and schools, particularly representing that golden age of choral music, the two centuries 1550-1750.

E. H. Wilcox

John Smallman

CONTENTS

MUSICAL CONTENTS

Chapter I

THE REHEARSAL HOUR

Successful rehearsals are based upon preparations which cover every detail of the rehearsal.

It is essential that the singers be alive physically and alert mentally. Every item which will assist toward this end must be considered.

Ventilation is an important factor in the rehearsal hour. Fresh air makes breathing easier, is conducive to sustaining the pitch, dissipates physical exhaustion, improves the spirit and is good for the health. This point must be considered particularly in small rooms where there is danger of drafts. Open the windows at their tops, or place screens in front of them if necessary to stop drafts. An attempt to sing in a room where the air is foul and stagnant will lead to flatting, poor tone quality, and dullness of spirit.

Lighting must be adequate. If the light is too bright, there is a glare which is tiring, and insufficient light is depressing. The right amount of indirect lighting will help to establish the proper mood for an enjoyable rehearsal. The light should be placed so that it shines on the music and on the conductor's face and hands.

Rehearsal rooms vary in acoustics. The ideal room for singing has enough resonance to give brilliance but without a confusing echo. In an oblong room, stand at one end and sing the length of the room. Each singer should be able to hear all the other voices in the chorus.

The general appearance of the room will affect the mental attitude of the chorus during the rehearsal. The room must be clean and its appearance must show attention to details. It is easier to sing in a beautiful room than in a barn. Nice surroundings stimulate nice responses. The conductor and the singers ought to feel a responsibility for the appearance of the rehearsal room so that it may be conducive to the spirit of song.

If there is a choice of hours, select the time at which the singers are apt to be fresh physically and mentally. The most will be accomplished when the singers are in the proper condition to expend maximum energy in the rehearsals. If the day is begun with song, it will improve the mental attitude throughout the day and thereby assist in all activities of the day.

A happy mental attitude is essential for good singing. Rehearsals are to be enjoyed. Little can be accomplished if rehearsals are drudgery. The right kind of singing leads to happiness, and a happy spirit makes singing easier.

1

Singers and conductor will resolve to accomplish something tangible each rehearsal. It is not sufficient merely to sing for the stipulated amount of time, even though the singing is thoroughly enjoyed. At the beginning of each rehearsal the conductor and singers must look forward to attaining certain definite results during the rehearsal.

Efficiency requires orderliness and discipline in the conduct of the rehearsal. The conductor will plan exactly what is to be done during the hour. He will have outlined a series of points to be accomplished and he will decide approximately the number of minutes for each point. He will also decide the method to be used in presenting each of these points.

The thoroughness with which the conductor prepares for the rehearsal, the orderliness with which he conducts the rehearsal, and the eagerness with which the singers follow his directions will determine to a large extent the success of the chorus. Given two groups of equal ability and experience, with two conductors of similar skill, except that one gets thirty minutes of actual work from an hour rehearsal, and the other gets fully sixty minutes from a similar hour rehearsal, it is easy to see which group will progress more rapidly. Many a mediocre conductor has triumphed over a rival of greater musical training, through using common sense in planning an efficient use of time in rehearsal.

Members of the chorus have much to do with the success of their organization by insisting on complete attention to the conductor. Talking, whispering, joking, or laughing among the members should never be tolerated except as sanctioned by the conductor. The experienced conductor will know when to permit a few minutes for a hearty laugh. A slight period for relaxation of this kind may help the singers to return to the music with renewed energy.

Chapter II

BREATHING

CORRECT breathing is attained when the singer has sufficient breath for all purposes, at all times, without strain or excess of effort. It is difficult to produce a good tone when the lungs are almost empty. The best tone is produced with the lungs fairly well inflated. This gives a pad of air behind the tone. Consequently the breathing must be developed to a point at which the entire capacity of the lungs is never fully required. The end of a phrase should be reached with air to spare.

The technical features of good breathing include:—

1. Unhampered, easy inhalation.

2. Abundance of air without strain at the end of inhalation.

3. Easy control of exhalation from slighest *pianissimo* to strongest *fortissimo*.

4. A surplus residue of air when new breath is taken so that the volume is never completely exhausted.

5. All degrees of sound emission, from a sustained unwavering *legato* to a completely detached *staccato*.

To attain poise of body, stand easily in an erect position with heels slightly apart and the right foot slightly ahead of the left in a position from which one can rise to his toes easily as though moving forward and approaching the audience. This is the posture of assurance. The weight is on the ball of the right foot.

The shoulders are expected to be loose as they sustain the weight of the upper arms hanging from the shoulders without effort.

The head will be at a point of attention with the chin neither elevated nor depressed but held in a position to give maximum freedom and ease of movement to the neck and lower jaw.

The upper part of the chest is expanded at the sides and front, and the front of the chest is raised toward the chin without tightening or crowding the neck. The shoulders must remain motionless. The feeling of expansion will be pleasant as when one takes joy in stretching a healthy muscle.

Natural breathing is correct breathing. It consists of four acts:—

1. Complete inhalation which fills the farthest recesses of the lungs around the lower ribs and waist at the sides and back without obtruding the abdomen. The chest and shoulders remain in a normal position. The feeling of expansion is greatest around the back and sides of the waist, where the singer can feel that he is inflating like a toad.

3

2. A moment of retaining the point of complete inhalation, while the singer is conscious of a feeling of buoyancy and expansion, which is now held without change by the diaphragm.

3. Exhalation which comes from the diaphragm and gives the feeling of pushing the air from the body by the muscles around the waist without moving the chest or shoulders.

4. A period of rest while the lungs are entirely empty and there is a feeling of complete collapse and relaxation about the breathing organs.

CHAPTER III

BREATHING EXERCISES

BREATHING exercises can well occupy ten minutes at the beginning of a sixty minute rehearsal. The exercises given in this chapter utilize singing from the very start. They are designed for group use. The singers should stand in rows without crowding. The conductor will count for the class at the rate of M.M. 60, and signal when each exercise is to end. Unless the conductor is at the piano or organ, he can move about among the members of the group, giving any necessary suggestions about posture, relaxation of shoulders or jaw, or pronunciation.

Rhythmic breathing consists of eight counts (four counts of rest at the point of complete exhalation and four of inhalation), followed by a tone or exercise to be sung as many counts as possible.

At the beginning of each series of exercises there is a preliminary act. Each exercise is sung several times in succession and this introductory routine is not used between the repetitions of the exercise.

The preliminary act consists of exhaling all the air from the lungs, vigorously as when one blows out candles on a birthday cake. This must be done with a positive physical effort as though the lungs were being thrown into a state of collapse. All muscles are relaxed in this process, but the original posture with raised chest is retained.

When this posture of exhalation is attained, the exercise begins, the first two acts occupying four counts each, and the third consuming as long as possible, in the following manner:—

1. Count four while remaining in a relaxed position with no air in the lungs.

2. Count four while inhaling slowly by expanding the diaphragm around the waist and especially at the lower ribs at the side and back, without protruding the abdomen.

3. Sing one of the exercises given on page 6, holding the final tone as long as possible without struggling. At the end of the tone the singer will be at the end of exhalation. Now begin again with the first act by holding this point of exhalation for four counts. Continue on through this exercise and repeat it several times.

Now begin the exercise again, starting with the preliminary act and singing the exercise at a pitch one-half step higher than previously. Repeat this exercise several times.

Raise the exercise by half-steps until it is sung five half-steps above the original pitch, then come back down to the original pitch, by half-steps. This will make eleven sections for the exercise.

When the first exercise has been sung at the various pitches indicated, take a minute's rest and move on to the second exercise which is to be sung with the same number of repeats at five pitches above the original key.

Exercise 1.
Syllable *n–n–ee*, pronounced the same as *knee*.
Sing *n–n–ee*.

Conductor
count—   1   2   3   4   1   2   3   4   1234 etc.   to the end of the breath.

In singing this syllable the *n* sound should be permitted to vibrate. The *n* sound begins before the beat in order to establish resonance and place the vowel against the teeth. It is probably impossible to exaggerate the *n* sound. It must be sung with much energy, to make the tone spin and to overcome the inertia of inadequate tone production. This is preparation for the vowel sound *ee* which begins on the beat.

Listen accurately to this vowel sound. The singer will listen to the vowel sound produced by his neighbors. If the pronunciations are all identical the tone for the whole group will form a blend which makes a single composite tone from the entire chorus.

Exercise 2.
Syllable *n–n–ay*, pronounced the same as *neigh*.
Sing *n–n–ay*.

Exercise 3.
Syllable *n–n–ah*, the vowel sound the same as the sighing sound *ah*.
Sing *n–n–ah*.

Exercise 4.
Syllable *n–n–oh*, pronounced the same as the word *know*.
Sing *n–n–oh*.

Chapter IV

A CAPPELLA SINGING

A true instrumental accompaniment will supply additional voices, increase the pitch range, add variety of tone quality, give amplified dynamic scope and extend the gamut of expression. The value of an accompaniment can be judged by the way it meets these points.

A piano "accompaniment" which merely duplicates the voice parts is of no value musically, although it may be useful to some choruses when they begin the study of a piece.

A chorus which cannot sing in tune without a piano or organ to play the voice parts, cannot sing in tune when an instrument is used. The sound of a chorus sagging below pitch and clinging desperately beneath the underside of the piano pitch is one of the most dismal experiences in music. It is better to discard the piano and permit the chorus to flat, because under these conditions some chords and some short passages may be in tune, whereas nothing is in tune when the chorus is dangling in mid-air from the piano pitch.

Even if the chorus sings in tune, the mixture of piano tone duplicating the voice parts hampers the blend, obscures the voice leadings, gives percussive effects when none are desired and interferes with many nuances.

Singers listen more attentively, develop more self-reliance, and sing with more accuracy and assurance when they are not trying to follow their parts as played on the piano.

Choruses should not limit themselves to either accompanied or unaccompanied singing. An *a cappella* chorus will profit by occasional excursions into other fields such as the oratorio repertoire with orchestral accompaniment. A church choir, accustomed to the organ, will do well to devote considerable time to unaccompanied singing. There is a temptation to shift too much responsibility to the piano or organ and use it beyond reason or necessity. Refinements of vocal tone and vocal style are developed most readily in unaccompanied polyphonic music.

If the piano or organ has a true accompaniment, use it. If it has merely a duplication of the voice parts, reduced to two staves, get on without it as soon as possible.

All of the compositions in this book have piano reductions of the voice parts. Use them if necessary when beginning the study of a piece, but eliminate them as soon as possible. All of this choral music is complete in itself as sung by voices alone. Only this *a cappella* style of singing will give the greatest purity of blend, distinctness of voice leading, accuracy of chording, delicacy of nuance, and the maximum of ear-training for the singers.

7

Chapter V

PRONUNCIATION

PRONUNCIATION is one of the most important elements of singing. Yet it is the weakest feature with many choruses. A group of limited talent can become a surprisingly good chorus through attention to this one element of good singing.

Accurate pronunciation requires accurate and intense listening. It involves close attention to details of sound. The lips and tongue will not pronounce words correctly unless the singer holds a vivid mental picture of the pronunciation desired. The sounds we speak or sing are reproductions of sounds which first exist in the mind. If the sound is inaccurate and slovenly, we can be sure the mental processes are inaccurate and slovenly also. As the ears become more alert and the mind becomes more observing, a singer's pronunciation becomes more accurate, pure and beautiful.

The speaking voice and the singing voice are identical as far as pronunciation is concerned. That is, we should sing with the same abandon we use in speech and with supreme accuracy of pronunciation. Singing is merely prolonged speaking. In singing, our chief difficulty with pronunciation is due to the inertia of the spoken language with our custom of speaking thoughtlessly and carelessly. Habits of speech affect singing, and singing should affect speech.

Pronunciation, as used in a very broad sense in this book, can be analyzed into three factors for the purpose of study. This three-fold division falls under the headings of vowels, consonants, and enunciation.

Vowels are the parts of words which are vocalized. Tone is sustained in the vowels. The quality of the tone and the singing lyric possibilities of the voice are determined largely by the way the vowels are handled. Resonance and evenness of scale are dependent upon the correct emission of the vowel sounds. Vowel sound may be considered the fundamental basic material of the singing voice.

Consonants add meaning and effect to the vowel sounds. They give significance and emotional content to words. They ride on the stream of vowel sound, punctuating it and making it more expressive. Consonants are the elements which put feeling and meaning into the flow of vowel sounds.

Enunciation refers to the methods of emitting syllables, words and sentences. It includes articulation and accent. Upon it rests the responsibility of making the text of the song clearly and distinctly intelligible to the listener with correct emphasis on the proper tones and syllables. Perfect enunciation is dependent on all the elements of good singing. Good enunciation will always lend expression to singing.

CHAPTER VI

PRIMARY VOWEL SOUNDS

THERE are four primary vowel sounds as used in the four exercises of Chapter III. Although in singing all shades of vowel quality are used, these various sounds are basically related to the four primary vowel sounds mentioned above. Every vowel sound in the English language has its source of life in one of these four.

In this chapter we shall discuss the four basic vowel sounds in their greatest purity. In a later chapter we shall consider the variations in vowel sounds which are limited to these four basic tonal-elements.

Although *ee* is a difficult vowel sound, it is extremely beneficial, and when correctly produced, it will feed the other vowels with resonance. We are accustomed to this vowel in such words as *lean*, *mean* and *kneel*. The beauty of these words is apparent when they are spoken vigorously and positively at the front of the mouth, with plenty of time to develop a spinning, concentrated and brilliant effect.

The tone produced in this vowel is most brilliant. The vowel *ee* is the most resonant vowel sound and produces the most concentrated tone. When properly sung, this vowel will give a spinning tone of dazzling beauty and great carrying power.

In singing this tone, the tip of the tongue will rest at the back of the lower teeth and the tongue will be arched. The facial muscles should be relaxed, permitting the lips to hang loose in front of the teeth. This forward position of the lips and facial muscles will produce a forward placement of the tone. The teeth should show as in smiling, but avoid making a grimace. This will help to give the tone a smiling, genial quality.

Avoid a hard, strident tone. This will not be difficult if the jaw, tongue, face, and neck are kept free and loose to assist the tone to issue free and unimpeded.

The *ay* sound is familiar to us in such words as *may*, *play*, *day*. It has more breadth and depth than *ee*. This vowel sound must be given its own very positive, definite quality. Otherwise it may sound like a cross between the true *ay* sound and the true *ee* sound. The end of the vowel sound *ay* is the sound *ee*, but the *ay* must be sustained through the length of the vowel, the *ee* appearing very lightly and quickly at the end of the principal vowel sound. But even this tinge of *ee* in the *ay* vowel sound tends to give it color and make the tone more brilliant. This is occasioned partly by the fact that *ee* is naturally focused at the front of the mouth. Anything which helps the *ay*

9

sound to be concentrated near the front of the mouth assists in giving brilliance and character to the *ay*.

The chief danger to avoid is the flannel sound which is muffled and dead in character, due to a failure to bring the tone forward in the mouth. The slight admixture of *ee* is a protection against this danger.

The *ah* sound is found in its typical form in the word *father*, especially when this word is pronounced lightly against the teeth. It is very important to smile while singing this vowel sound as the smile will eliminate the tendency to say *aw*. *Ah* is an expression of delight whereas *aw* is an expression of disappointment. In this vowel sound the mouth is open wide as though biting into a large apple. The mouth has a feeling of being wider than long. The tongue is absolutely flat or even concave. The throat is stretched wide. This sound opens the mouth and throat more than any other sound. With this wide open, relaxed position of the vocal organs, the sound can roll out easily and unimpeded with great beauty and power.

It is necessary to keep the resonance in the front part of the mouth with this vowel also. Do not give the impression of swallowing the tone.

Oh is a dangerous sound because of its tendency to be throaty or guttural. Maintain the same brilliant ring to this tone which is secured in the vowel sound *ee*, and this will give resonance and character to the vowel sound *oh*.

In Exercise 5 the two most brilliant vowel sounds are made to fuse into the *oh* sound with which the exercise closes. This is a splendid exercise to develop the ringing quality in the *oh* sound.

The four positions of throat, mouth, tongue and lips, as used in producing the four primary vowels: *ee*, *ay*, *ah*, *oh*, give the greatest resonance of which the vocal organs are capable. There are numerous other vowel sounds, produced with slightly different adjustments of the vocal organs, but none of them have the firm virility and warm resonance of the four primary vowel sounds as produced in these four primary positions of the vocal organs. Therefore it is wise, especially for the beginner, to produce these other vowel sounds which are described in later chapters, with the least possible variation from these four primary vocal positions. No matter what the vowel sound, retain a primary vocal position, and the tone will attain its maximum body and musical effectiveness.

Breath control and freedom of tongue, throat, and jaw are interdependent. One cannot be attained without the other. Neither will be secured without the proper position of the throat and mouth cavities to resonate the tone and place the voice in the fore part of the mouth against the teeth. This is the fundamental principle underlying voice production.

In all study of singing, the ear must be the constant guide and supreme judge. References to mouth positions and other physical factors must be considered as hints to help the vocal organ in its search for a way to satisfy the requirements of the ear. In learning to sing, psychology is always more important than physiology.

EXERCISE 5

Chapter VII

COMBINATIONS OF PRIMARY VOWEL SOUNDS

COMBINATIONS of primary vowel sounds are known as compound or double vowels.

When two vowel sounds appear in immediate succession, making a compound vowel, there is a point of confusion and indistinctness while the tone is changing from one vowel sound to its successor. During this change the sound is indefinite and unpleasant. Consequently, it is necessary to move as quickly as possible from one vowel sound to another.

It is also essential to determine at what place in a sustained tone the shift from one vowel to another shall occur. In most cases it is best to sustain the first vowel sound to the end of the note or notes and then glide imperceptibly and quickly into the second vowel sound, allowing it the shortest possible space of time. This gives practically the entire value of the note to the first vowel.

The *i* sound as in *light* is a very common compound vowel. It consists of the two primary vowel sounds, *ah* and *ee*. This sound is not always spelled with an *i*, for example: *aye, eye, fortify, lie*. In all these cases the long sound is related to the primary sound *ah* which is sustained for the entire length of the tone, with a quick glide to the *ee* at the very end.

The diphthong *ou* as in *out*, *thou*, and the sound *ow* as in *now*, are equivalent to *ah* and *oo*. This sound may be sustained in a very clear *ah*. The *oo* sound at the end must be treated lightly and quickly and contain within it a good deal of the *oh* sound, as explained on page 14.

The diphthong *oi* as in *joy* and *rejoice* is equivalent to *aw* and *ee*. The *aw* sound is sustained for the entire duration of the tone. In itself, it is a hybrid tone, based upon the fundamental vowel sound *ah*, but with a tinge of *oh* added, so that it is midway between these two primary vowel sounds.

In contrast to the combinations mentioned above, we now have a compound vowel in which the order is reversed: the first vowel is given very short duration, the shift to the second vowel being made as soon and as rapidly as possible in order to give it the full value of the note. This is long *u* as in *few* and *dew*. It is equivalent to *ee* and *oo*. The *ee* sound is passed over quickly and the duration of the tone devoted entirely to the *oo* which has its own difficulties, as explained on page 14. No matter what vowel sound is being held, it must be sustained purely and distinctly without change of quality. A slow change from one vowel sound to another gives a hideous effect which is useful only in imitating the nocturnal call of cats.

The ability to sustain a clear, definite vowel without change of quality is absolutely essential when several tones are to be sung on one syllable with the same warmth and resonance on each tone.

Chapter VIII

VARIATIONS OF PRIMARY VOWEL SOUNDS

Each primary vowel sound, when properly produced, is dependent upon a definite position of the mouth and throat cavities to give the tone resonance, strength, quality, and beauty. The shape of the mouth and throat cavities is determined by the position of the tongue, the jaw, the lips, and the muscles of the throat. There is only one position of these organs which will give the maximum assistance to a certain vowel sound. The first problem of the singer is to find this position and retain it through the duration of the tone.

As there are four primary vowel sounds, there will be four primary positions for the mouth and throat cavities. All other vowel sounds are related to the primary vowel sounds. These other vowel sounds which are variations of the primary vowels have a tendency to distort the mouth and throat cavities from the four primary resonating positions, and by doing this, the resonance is hampered and the tones produced lack character, warmth, brilliance, and power. From the musical standpoint it is wise to relate these variation vowel sounds to the primary vowels with which they are grouped by adjusting the mouth and throat cavities to approximate one of the primary positions, while producing variation vowel sounds. This will give resonance and character to these variation vowel sounds.

Ee is the primary vowel for the short *i* as found in the words *in, is, if, with*. In these sounds the mouth has a tendency to spread too wide, producing a dull, colorless tone with no character or resonance. Sometimes this sound will become more like the short *e* if the singer is not careful.

To produce the tone correctly for vocal purposes, use the same voice equipment which is used for the *ee*. Do not hold the mouth any wider than for *ee*. Hold the focus of the tone at the front of the mouth for producing a spinning, concentrated, virile tone, such as we associate with the tone *ee*. This admixture of the primary vowel element into this variation vowel sound will give it color, carrying power and effectiveness.

Ay is the primary vowel for the short *e* sound as in *rest, hideth, then, there* and *where*.

In this variation vowel sound there is danger of not opening the mouth wide enough. Maintain the vocal position used for *ay*. This will give nobility and breadth to the short *e* sound.

Ah is the basis for the short *a* as in *ran, and, laugh*. This sound has a tendency to be nasal, thin, and unpleasant. But if the mouth position for the primary sound *ah* is retained, the *a* sound can never become nasal, white, and repulsive.

Such words as *thanks* have a tendency to lack dignity and beauty. The mind moves on from the short *a* sound to the *nks* too rapidly, and this produces confusion in the vowel sound. Hold the short *a* for the full duration of the tone, thinking only *a* and maintaining the position for its primary vowel sound *ah*. The *nks* will then enter quickly at the end of the tone without distorting the vowel sound.

Avoid exaggeration of this policy in such words as *and*. This word must be formed in the position of the primary vowel sound *ah*, but it should not be distorted into the sound *awnd*.

The short *u* sound as in *sun*, *run*, *fun*, and *done*, is usually held in relationship to *ah*.

Oh is the primary basic sound for the short *oo* sound, found in *moon*, *soon*. In these sounds there is a tendency to contract the throat until it becomes a narrow tube with no opportunity for the sound to resonate and develop character of tone. The result is a sound like the cooing of a dove. It is a mooing sound because it contains nothing but the high head voice with no resonance from the lower resonating cavities. If the vocal position for the vowel sound *oh* is retained in mind while singing the variation sound *oo*, the tone produced will have more resonance and character.

Chapter IX

CONSONANTS

"A CONSONANT is a letter which represents an impression made upon the mind when the sound is abruptly, markedly, or forcibly stopped by the lips, teeth, nose, or palate." (Coward)

Good articulation is impossible without precise, clear-cut consonants. Consonants give meaning and emotion to the flow of sound based on the vowels. Care must be taken that each consonant be emitted with exactly the stress required and with the proper speed or duration to make the words accurate and distinct.

Some consonants are resonant. We have used *m* and *n* in our first exercises because of their resonance. Other classes of consonants have no resonance whatever. The sounds *s* and *t* are examples of this class of consonants.

In the case of consonants which have resonance, we may wish to give appreciable time-value to the consonants, but in the cases which have no resonance, the time-value will be limited to the least possible.

There are seven classes of consonants, determined by the place at which the sound is stopped. The tone is never interrupted in the mouth cavity. The points of stoppage are at the front of the mouth, in the teeth and lips, or behind the mouth, in the throat, palate, or nose.

Labial consonants are *v*, *w*, *b*, and *p*. *V* has considerable resonance. *W* and *b* are also resonant, but *p* has no resonance whatever.

The dental consonants are *d* and *t*, the only difference between them being that the former has resonance and the latter has none. If the *d* is produced in a slovenly manner, without due attention to its resonating quality, it will sound like *t*. In that case the word *Lord* will sound like *lort*.

The palatal consonants are *l*, *r*, *j* and *ch*. *L* and *r* are decidedly resonant. *J* has some resonance which must be brought out adequately or it will sound like *ch* which has no resonance.

The nasal consonants are *m* and *n*. These are the two most resonant consonants we have. They induce vibration throughout the whole mechanism, but particularly in the resonating chambers of the head.

The guttural consonants are hard *g* and *k*. The former has resonance but the latter has none.

The aspirates·are *h* and *q*, sung rapidly without resonance.

15

The sibilants are *s*, *z*, and *ce* at the end of a word. The *z* has resonance but the others are merely hisses and should be sung as rapidly as possible, particularly when they come at the end of a word. Otherwise the sustained hissing of the chorus will give a ludicrous effect.

Certain consonants are discovered with or without resonance, depending upon the way they are produced. *Th* in the word *thought* is used with a soft production and has no resonance. *Th* in the word *thine* has the hard production which requires resonance.

Some of the most resonant consonants are occasionally classed in one group as the liquid sounds: *m*, *n*, *l*, *r*, and *v*. R demands particular attention because it requires various treatments, depending upon the position it occupies in the word. When *r* is followed by the vowel it may be rolled. When *r* is at the beginning of a word, it is rolled with great strength. If it is in the middle of the word, it has less strength, and if it is at the end of the word, it is eliminated almost entirely. This must be observed in such words as *father, mother, teacher.*

All resonant consonants have a definite pitch. When such a consonant precedes the vowel sound of a syllable, the pitch of the consonant must be the same as the pitch of the following vowel sound.

The consonant should precede the time-value for the note written, so that the vowel sound will begin at the time indicated for the note. If the consonant has been sung at the proper pitch for the following vowel, it will assist the singer to remain at the proper pitch. The pitch given to initial vowels has much to do with good intonation from the chorus.

Final consonants which have resonance must retain the same pitch as the preceding vowel sound. The following exercises are intended to energize the consonant. There is a tendency for the singer to be lax in the production of these consonant sounds. The tongue must be released quickly from the palate to produce the vowel, and immediately rebound to the former position on the palate to continue the consonant. Greater breath pressure will be required for the consonants than for the vowel sounds.

Practice of these exercises will lead one to sing such words as *hosanna* with exuberance, occasioned by the resonance in the *san* which is stressed and given full value.

EXERCISE 6

Ll- ee- ll- ee- ll- ee- ll- ee- ll- ee ___
Ll- ay- ll- ay- ll- ay- ll- ay- ll- ay ___
Ll- ah- ll- ah- ll- ah- ll- ah- ll- ah ___
Ll- oh- ll- oh- ll- oh- ll- oh- ll- oh ___

Exercise 7

Nn-ee-nn-ee-nn-ee-nn-ee-nn-ee
Nn-ay-nn-ay-nn-ay-nn-ay-nn-ay
Nn-ah-nn-ah-nn-ah-nn-ah-nn-ah
Nn-oh-nn-oh-nn-oh-nn-oh-nn-oh

Exercise 8

Mm-ee-mm-ee-mm-ee-mm-ee-mm-ee
Mm-ay-mm-ay-mm-ay-mm-ay-mm-ay
Mm-ah-mm-ah-mm-ah-mm-ah-mm-ah
Mm-oh-mm-oh-mm-oh-mm-oh-mm-oh

These exercises can be transposed upward and downward by half-steps to make a series of exercises, the extent of which will be determined by the range of the voices.

Chapter X

VOWELS INTRODUCED BY CONSONANTS

Ave Verum Corpus—William Byrd (1543-1623)

AVE VERUM CORPUS is a beautiful piece of music which gives excellent opportunities to study several problems of choral singing. Only a few of the most obvious and fundamental problems will be listed here. Difficulties of lesser importance will crop up in nearly every measure.

Just below the text the phonetic spelling for each word is given. The part of the word to sustain is outside of the parenthesis. The part of the word which is sung quickly is within the parenthesis. These latter are the sounds and letters which interrupt the smooth flow of tone or produce unpleasant changes in the vowel sound while it is being sustained. The letters in parenthesis must be given particular attention in order that they may be emitted precisely, distinctly and rapidly. This will bring each word clearly to the ears of the listener without impairing the beauty and continuity of the flow of the stream of vowels.

Below the phonetic spelling you will find the primary vowel sounds on which the positions of the throat and mouth are based, as explained in Chapters VI and VIII. It is interesting to note that the vowels of the Latin are all exactly in one of the four basic positions, with only two exceptions. This indicates one reason why Italian is a grateful language to sing. The two exceptions are *eh*, a variation of the *ay* position, and *oo*, a variation of the *oh* position.

There is no English sound which exactly duplicates the Italian pronunciation of long *e* in Latin. In this text we indicate the sound of Italian long *e* by *ay* without the final vanish sound *ee*. The sound must be darker and more intense than *eh* but it must avoid the final sound of the compound vowel *ay–ee* which is used so commonly by English-speaking people.

When using the English language, our voices are hampered by habits to which we have become accustomed in the careless speech of the streets. The Italian-Latin pronunciation will be used for the purpose of vocalization because it is more liquid and singable.

This composition is particularly useful as a study in pronunciation. We will give ear especially to the way vowels are introduced by consonants at the same pitch.

The problem of perfect pitch can be simplified by approaching the vowel sounds correctly through the preceding consonant. In the following piece, the second syllable of the first word is introduced by the consonant *v*. This must be approached on the pitch of the following vowel sound *ay*. The second word begins with the syllable "*ve*," and the *v* must be formed on the pitch of the vowel sound for this syllable. The second syllable of this word is "*rum*." The *r* will establish the pitch for the following *oom*. Accurate attention to the introduction of vowel sounds through consonants which precede them, without change of pitch, will do much to solve the problem of poor intonation. The slovenly habit of permitting consonants to be sung at any pitch, dictated by chance, between the preceding and succeeding vowel sounds, always leads to grief.

When accurate pronunciation is attained for each word, the blend among the various voices on each part will be improved. No matter how large the chorus or how many voices are used on each part, close attention must be given to producing a blend which will make all the voices on each part weld into one single rich tone.

Although accurate pronunciation is the chief factor in securing blend, there is another important point to consider. One voice with a tremolo can destroy the blend of all voices with which it is associated. The ideal voice for choral singing produces a "straight line" tone. This makes it possible to tune accurately to a perfect unison in each part. Thus a perfect blend is dependent upon smoothly sustained voices without a wobble, and accurate pronunciation. When a perfect blend is attained, it is possible to hear intonation accurately, thereby maintaining the pitch. If accurate intonation is to be secured, the pitch of each part must be easily and distinctly apparent to the ear. A chorus producing a jumble of sound with no blend of voices and no attention to unity of pronunciation can never sing in tune.

Simple examples of the art of contrapuntal singing are to be found in this number. Contrapuntal music is essentially music in which every voice has a part of melodic interest. Often an important melodic bit is sung first by one voice and then by another, proving that all voices are of equal importance. This is imitational singing. It is characteristic of the best polyphonic (many voiced) or contrapuntal music. It is great fun to see that these imitations are exact and significant. In measures 24-27 the tenor voice sings a melodic fragment on the words "*in cruce*." The soprano sings this same fragment, beginning one measure later. In measures 37-40 the alto sings a very important solo phrase on the words "*unda fluxit*." The soprano sings this same phrase beginning with measure 38 but using a different pitch. The bass voice makes an entrance in measure 39, imitating what the alto did two measures before. The tenor, in measure 40, begins this same phrase on the same pitch used for the soprano. We could say the soprano replies to the alto and the tenor replies to the bass. Each of these parts is a solo part (sung by all voices assigned to the part, of course) and needs to be treated accordingly. There must be a very decided entrance by each of these parts in order that it may stand out. The first note of each solo is marked accented. It is a general rule that the entrance of any part in an imitative passage of this sort will be sung positively and with an accent at the beginning. This brings the part to the listener's ears in a way to command attention. After a positive entry of this kind, the part usually subsides somewhat to give the following voice opportunity to make a prominent entry. This is particularly true when the melody is moving downward.

Beginning with measure 72, we have an excellent example of voices imitating each other in a rhythmical motive. The altos and tenors sing this motive covering two measures. In measure 74, the bass enters with the same motive and the soprano replies in measure 75. In measure 76, the alto starts the motive. In measure 77, the tenor begins it. In measure 78, the alto begins again and in measure 80 the soprano has it. The bass introduces this same motive starting on the last half of measure 81 and the tenor introduces it again in measure 83. This motive with slight variation is heard 22 times in this piece. Obviously, it should always be sung in the same style. When it first appears in measures 72-73, it is sung with a swell which reaches its height on the third syllable of the word *"miserere."* In nearly every case this starts with the bar line so that the point of greatest swell is at the beginning of the second measure, and the final syllable of the word, which is now dying away, is on the unaccented latter part of the measure. But in measure 81 the bass enters on the last half of the measure. This throws the climax of the swell on the last half of the following measure, and puts the final unaccented syllable of the word *"miserere"* on the first beat of measure 83. At first glance this would seem to alter the accents in the melody, but the melody is more important than the bar lines and the basses must sing this melody with the same accents used by the previous voices which have entered at the beginning of the measure. In fact, when this number was written, bar lines had not yet become the harsh dictators they oftentimes were in the nineteenth century, and each voice was expected to sing its part expressively, stressing the long tones and important words, and imitating those who have sung the same melody earlier in the piece. This rhythmic independence of voices is one of the characteristics of the finest choral music.

"Ave verum corpus"

In preparing for the initial vowel sound, take a deep breath and leave the throat open as in yawning before starting the tone. After

drawing the breath, it is quite important to suspend action for a moment with the entire vocal mechanism in the proper position to sing
the vowel at the pitch indicated.   This not only adjusts and relaxes
the vocal mechanism but makes it possible for all voices to open the
tone simultaneously.   Avoid the pinched attack which gives rise to
the "stroke of the glottis."   There will be little danger of this if the
action is suspended for a moment with the lungs inflated, the throat
open, and the jaws and tongue relaxed before the tone is emitted.
Hold the tone steady with no tremolo and merely a slight increase in
volume for the four beats of the two measures.   When moving to the
third measure, be careful to place the pitch of the *v* without slurring
downward.   In the word "*verum*" the *r* will again determine the pitch.
The tone swells through measure 4 to its climax at the beginning of
measure 5.   All voices must swell to the same extent in order to keep
the chord properly balanced.   The tenor will accent firmly at the
beginning of measure 5 and sustain his tone with a swell into the next
measure, thus carrying over the gap while the others are breathing
at the end of measure 5.   Notice that the bass has F♮ in measure 4 in
contrast to the F♯ of the soprano in the previous measure.   On the
syllable "*rum*," it is advisable to roll the *r*.   This must be done with
a very light pressure and relaxed tongue.   The *r* will, of course, be
rolled on the pitch of the following vowel sound.

The *decrescendo* from the peak of the swell is difficult to produce
correctly.   Do not have too much *decrescendo* at first.   There is always
a tendency to diminish from *mf* to *p* in one measure, and then to take
three measures to diminish from *p* to *pp*.   In a *crescendo*, do not start
to build up too soon.   The artistic control of a well balanced swell
by an entire chorus is very difficult to obtain, but it is worth contin-
uous effort.   The first nine measures of this number give plenty of
opportunity for practice on an artistic swell.

When the sopranos sing "*corpus*" they will find it necessary to
make a slight accent by breath pressure on the tone *G* which is the
second note on the syllable "*cor*."   The two eighth-notes should be
slightly detached in order that they may stand out distinctly.   It is
often necessary to detach eighth-notes slightly when they are sounding
against a sustained chord in order to have them sound perfectly clear,
with a distinct repetition of the vowel sound on the second note.

On the final syllable, "*pus*," use a firm pressure of the lips in making the *p*, and be sure it establishes the pitch for the following chord.
In this chord the tenor part is marked slightly louder than the other
voices because this tone determines the character of the chord.   The
ear might expect B♭, which would produce a minor triad, but the
composer has written B♮, which gives the major triad.   There must
be no doubt as to whether the tenors are singing B♭ or B♮.   The pitch

must be definitely up to B♮, and they must all sing this tone in tune so it will sound out distinctly. This final tone is taken very softly but the tone must not be flabby. Hold the vowel concentrated and pointed although sustained softly. Bear in mind that it must have the spinning, resonant quality which will make it audible in the farthest corner of the concert hall, while still soft where the singers are standing. This phrase is followed by an opportunity for a deep, slow breath.

"Natum de Maria Virgine"

This phrase is built much like the previous one and consists of a single extended swell. But it is deeply charged with emotion and feeling, whereas the first phrase is ethereal in effect. This second phrase takes on a more vigorous, red-blooded quality. It does not begin quite so softly as the previous phrase, and it builds to a louder and more imposing climax.

There must be a strong preliminary *n* before the down-beat which should be tuned accurately in order that the following vowel sound may be in tune. The second syllable of the first word is finished with a strong *m* sound. When the basses skip upward an octave in measure 11, they accent the word "*de*." This is the point at which the main *crescendo* begins, the previous measure and a half having been sustained with little increase in sound. In measure 12, both syllables are pronounced positively with an increase in tone leading up to a firm chord in measure 13. The *r* in "*Maria*" must be strongly rolled at the pitch of the ensuing vowel sound to give it life. The *ee* should be sung with great brilliance and virility.

Remember that *v* in the word "*Virgine*" has a pitch which must be properly approached. When the bass starts this word, the climax of the swell is reached and there is a gradual *diminuendo* through the following measures. The bass must sing the eighth-notes distinctly and somewhat detached. In the last half of measure 15, some or all of the basses may drop down an octave as the composer originally intended. There will be a slight accent on the low *G* for the bass and the other voices will sing the quarter-note after this low *G* has been firmly established. The upper three voices can give a slight throb to the tone where the dot holds them sustained as the bass drops to this low *G*.

"Vere passum"

This is a short phrase containing a short swell and ending very softly. The whole color of this phrase is dark in contrast to the brightness of the preceding phrase. It is cathedral-like in quality and the word "*passum*" is sung as a soft prayer. The bass will sustain its final syllable while the other voices breathe, preparatory to beginning the next word.

"Immolatum"

This word covers another short phrase in a short swell. The first vowel sound, although soft, should be accented and should be sung as a very resonant *ee*. Remember that *m* and *l* have pitch which is determined by the succeeding vowel sounds. Note that the *m* sound appears only as a preliminary to the *oh*, the preceding syllable consisting of *ee* alone without any *m* sound. There is excellent opportunity for tuning at this point. The bass and tenor have the octave *C* which can be easily tuned at the end of measure 22. At the beginning of measure 23, the alto and bass should tune the octave *F*. As the tenor moves down to the *F* held by the basses, it can be tuned to a perfect unison, and then the basses with the lowest voices can drop down a perfect octave to the *F* at the beginning of measure 24, as indicated by the small note. Some of the basses will retain the *F* on the fourth line, only those with particularly deep voices being requested to take the low *F*. In fact, it is not necessary that any voices sing this low *F* if it is not comfortable.

"In cruce pro homine"

This is the beginning of the imitational singing referred to on page 19. Each voice will sing the word *"in"* with a firm resonant vowel sound, avoiding the "stroke of the glottis." The word *"pro"* has a rolled *r*. There is a strong aspirate on the syllable *"ho."* The bass will give an accent on the beginning of measure 29 where he sings E♭ against the *D* of the alto, making a discord which is held firmly by the alto until it resolves to a sweet concord on the last half of the measure.

The tenor has a difficult part beginning with the last half of measure 27. He sings the word *"pro"* distinctly and positively and enters measure 28 with an accent on the syllable *"ho."* This must be sustained firmly over into the last half of the measure, giving the other three voices opportunity to breathe and start the new chord while he is sustaining the top tone. He then moves down an octave, quickly and neatly, without *glissando*, and follows this with a new tone at the beginning of measure 29, these three pitches all being on one unchanged vowel sound. In measure 29 the altos and tenors pronounce the syllable *"mi"* simultaneously while the sopranos and basses sustain the previous chord and wait until the last quarter-note in the measure to pronounce the syllable *"mi."* This phrase ends with a *diminuendo* and a soft cadence.

"Cujus latus"

This phrase calls for a masculine attack and steady, firm, *forte* treatment of the four chords. There must be no release of pressure on these four chords except that the final syllable is shortened for purposes of phrasing. This also separates the final *s* sound from the beginning consonant of the following phrase.

"*Perforatum*"

This phrase begins firmly and diminishes to *mf* to prepare for the contrapuntal entrance of the voices in the following phrase, without permitting a complete relaxation. The *r* is rolled only on the third syllable "*ra.*" Avoid the *r* in the first syllable.

"*Unda fluxit sanguine*"

The entrances of the voices have been described above. Listen intently to the vowel sounds. In singing *forte* do not neglect the same refinements of listening and tone production of which you are capable on the soft tones. The syllable "*un*" must be sung with open throat and a round full tone. The word "*sanguine*" must be sung with much suppressed feeling. This word is sung in a very smooth legato manner with no interruption between the syllables. The soprano and alto repeat the word. Each prepares for the second entrance of the word by completing its first pronunciation in time to take a breath and enter exactly on the beat. This point needs to be watched by the sopranos in particular.

"*Esto nobis*"

This phrase is similar to the one on "*cujus latus.*" It is bright and hopeful in contrast to the previous phrase. It is sung firmly and *forte* with no release between the chords. The final "*bis*" will need to be shortened to make a graceful close for the phrase and to make a release between the end of this phrase and the beginning of the phrase following. This will also give opportunity to complete the *s* before taking up the *p* sound.

"*Praegustatum*"

The *r* should be rolled. Let the tenor hold the syllable "*bis*" firmly until the new syllable is sounding clearly in the other voices. The whole phrase is firm but the cadence at the end is completed gracefully, the upper three voices taking a short breath before the entrance of the succeeding phrase.

"*In mortis examine*"

This is very sombre in character. It has no decided accent. The tones should be dark throughout. Breathing places are indicated at points which make it possible to complete the syllable "*tis*" and then take up the new syllable "*ex*" without confusion. Pay particular attention to the final cadence where the $B\flat$ in the soprano part is tied over and then moves down to *A* before resolving to the final *B♭*. The alto is held on *F* until the last quarter of the measure, then it moves down to *E♭* on its way to *D*.

"*O dulcis*"

This must be sung very sweetly and tenderly. The soprano will strive for a pure flute-like quality of tone. The other voices will sing smoothly, striving for perfect blend, accurate intonation and an even swell so that their parts form a chord which seems to echo the soprano. The tenor must be careful to sing the *B♮* up close to *C*, and the three lower voices must close the chord exactly together. This is another place in which the low basses may sing the small low notes.

"*O pie*"

Although this is an imitation of the previous phrase, it is even more pleading in character. Its quality is intensified in comparison with the previous four measures. Again the low basses may sing the small notes.

"*O Jesu, fili Mariae*"

This is taken slightly slower than the previous measure. There should be no accent on the syllable "*Je*" and the tender style is retained. The quarter-notes in the soprano and in the tenor at measures 67 and 70 are detached. The *r* in "*Mariae*" is rolled. Give particular attention to this cadence with the suspended alto part and the moving tenor.

"*Miserere mei*"

At this point the tempo increases to avoid any tendency to monotony and to make a proper setting for an artistic close with a return to the original tempo. This is a very smooth *legato* phrase. Fortunately there are no absolute consonants to interfere with the sustained flow of tone. The altos and tenors must set a good example by producing a well molded phrase, the two parts swelling and diminishing in equal amounts in order to obtain the proper balance.

In measures 74-75, where the bass sings his melody, he follows the melodic pattern established by the alto and tenor in the previous two measures. This necessitates his singing *F♮* in order to outline the proper melodic shape. The *F♮* is maintained even though the tenor is singing *F♯* throughout the measure. The same situation obtains in measures 81-83.

In measures 78-81 the bass will accent each half-note as his tone is related to the motive which is being repeated in all other voices. In measure 84 it will be necessary for the soprano to detach the quarter-notes and repeat the vowel sounds of the syllable being sung.

In the following two measures, treat the cadence carefully and very softly. The altos must guard their intonation to sing a pure $B\natural$. There is a slight *crescendo* on this chord which gives the first intimation of the approaching climax.

"*O dulcis*"

This will be sung in the same style as before, except that it is now slightly louder, approaching the climax.

"*O pie*"

This builds up still more with increased volume and a decided pleading, human quality.

"*O Jesu, fili Mariae*"

Here we attain the climax of the entire piece. It is sung with a strongly personal and human feeling. It is a desperate prayer to the Saviour. This is the most emotional phrase in the entire composition. On the word "*Mariae*," roll the *r* strongly.

"*Miserere mei*"

We now return to the same speed used at the beginning. The music gradually decreases in power, leading to a very quiet ending. The tenor is given the honor of stating for the last time the melody which has been repeated so often. He does this in measures 113-14 and he should be careful to give adequate stress to the quarter-note *C*. The final "*Amen*" is a test for breath control. On the long sustained tones, the singers must breathe individually at different times so there will be a continual flow of tone. This plan can be used for the soprano and bass, particularly on the final few measures of this lovely cadence.

The Latin text may be translated as follows—

Ave verum corpus
Hail true body

natum de Maria virgine;
born of Mary the virgin;

Vere passum, immolatum
Which has truly suffered

in cruce pro homine;
on the cross for man;

Cujus latus perforatum
Whose pierced side

unda fluxit sanguine;
flowed with blood;

Esto nobis praegustatum
May we receive Thee

in mortis examine.
in the ordeal of death.

O dulcis, O pie, O Jesu fili Mariae,
O sweet One, O kind One, O Jesus son of Mary,

miserere mei.   Amen.
have mercy on me.   Amen.

AVE VERUM CORPUS

Motet for Mixed Voices

Edited by John Smallman

WILLIAM BYRD (1543-1623)
Gradualia Lib.I 1605

77384-117

Soprano
-xit san - gui - ne, san - gui - ne; Es -
-ksee - (t) sah - (n) gwee - neh sah - (n) gwee - neh eh -
ee ah ee ay ah ee ay ay

Alto
xit san - gui - ne, san - gui - ne; Es -
ksee - (t) sah - (n) gwee - neh sah - gui - neh eh -
ee ah ee ay ah ee ay ay

Tenor
un - da flu - xit san - gui - ne; Es -
oo - (n) dah floo - ksee - (t) sah - (n) gwee - neh eh - (s)
oh ah oh ee ah ee ay ay

Bass
-da flu - - - xit san - gui - ne; Es -
-(n) dah floo - - - ksee - (t) sah - (n) gwee - neh eh -
ah oh ee ah ee ay ay

- to no - bis prae - gu - sta - tum in mor -
-(s) toh noh - bee-(s) pray - goo - stah - too-(m)ee - (n) moh -
oh oh ee ay oh ah oh ee oh

- to no - bis prae - gu - sta - tum in mor -
-(s) toh noh - bee-(s) pray - goo - stah - too-(m)ee - (n)moh - (r)
oh oh ee ay oh ah oh ee oh

to no - - bis prae - gu - sta - tum in mor -
toh noh - bee - (s) pray - goo - stah - too-(m)ee - (n) moh -
oh oh ee ay oh ah oh ee oh

- to no - bis prae - gu - sta - tum in
-(s) toh noh - bee-(s) pray - goo - stah - too - (m) ee-(n)
oh oh ee ay oh ah oh ee

* In measures 64 to 71 inclusive the original tenor and alto parts have been interchanged to relieve the alto of several low notes. Also in measures 94 to 101.

36

Chapter XI

TWO TONES ON ONE VOWEL SOUND

How Shall I Fitly Meet Thee?—Johann Sebastian Bach (1685-1750)

HOW *Shall I Fitly Meet Thee?* was a favorite choral with Bach. He used it several times in the *St. Matthew Passion* and repeated it in the new setting chosen for this book in the *Christmas Oratorio.*

This choral is imbued with a spirit of deepest reverence and sincerity. In mood it is a great question, asking how a man shall meet his God. The questioning spirit is maintained to the last, where it is amplified by a half-close on the dominant chord.

There are eight phrases of two measures each, six of which end with a fermata. The first and third phrases are identical musically as are the second and fourth. Thus the sixteen measures are reduced to twelve, yet in this short composition there is adequate opportunity for the expression of deep and noble feeling. Accuracy, clearness, frankness, sincerity, simplicity, dignity, and a restrained expression of deep feeling as found in this choral are characteristics of great art.

An effective method of rehearsing this number is based on a reading of the poem by the conductor, bringing out its meaning and significance. The choral can then be played from beginning to end with each person listening intently to his own part. The conductor will beat eight to the measure, giving one beat to each eighth-note,* and the quarter-notes† will be held to the full value of two beats, which gives plenty of opportunity for the sound to resonate. On second hearing, all voices may hum softly with the piano or organ. Care must be taken by each singer to secure adequate breath to carry each phrase through from beginning to end on one breath without exhausting the supply of air. The chorus is then ready to hum the number through without accompaniment. Considerable time can be given over to humming, paying great attention to the dynamics and the details of the music before the words are used. Even in performance, it has been found effective to hum the choral after the words have been sung, in order to make a longer number and deepen the impression.

The vowel sounds can all be reduced to the four primary vocal sounds as indicated in the text. This does not mean there are only four sounds required in this choral, for each of the basic sounds is subject to variations, all of which will give the greatest resonance with the position of the vocal organs which is nearest to the basic vowel sound position.

* or quaver   † or crotchets

37

The variations on the sound *ah* are numerous, even in this short piece. "Art," "dark," "heart," are words with a similar *ah* sound, but they are quite different in vowel sound from "shall," "that," "and," "as," which also are based on *ah*. If we chose the words "my," "right," "bright," "shine," "light," we would have another quality of *ah*. "Fount" and "upon" would introduce still different shades, yet they are all derived from the *ah* vocal position and give the greatest resonance when that position is most closely approximated.

In the second phrase on the second syllable of the word "welcome" the basic *oh* position is suggested. This position is to be recommended particularly for voices that are white or without color. But for sombre voices of the throaty variety, which are most often found among altos and basses, the *ah* basis will be more helpful.

On the following word, "due," pass quickly over the *ee* and sustain the *oo*, but in the third phrase on the word "to" avoid any affectation, such as *teeoo*. Open the throat by modelling the word on the vowel sound *oh*.

In the fifth phrase, in the words "light shine brightly" there is splendid opportunity to study the compound vowel *ah–ee* in three successive words. Be sure to sustain the *ah* for the entire value, passing quickly over the *ee* at the end of the sound.

The word "serve" on the third beat of the first measure of the seventh phrase, must be distinct, clear and definite. The *er* sound, if permitted to go to seed, will make a partition between the throat and the mouth. This kills the tone and gives a nasty sound. In order to hold the throat and mouth open, sing the word "serve" with the basic mouth position for the vowel *oh*.

The final word, "art," will be sung with attention to the *ah* sound, the *r* and *t* appearing very quickly and lightly at the extreme end of the tone.

The first phrase begins with the aspirate *h*. The escape of breath must be distinct but gentle, preceding the fourth beat so the vowel can begin on the fourth beat and have a full quarter-note value. In approaching this first word, the throat must be relaxed and open as it is when yawning.

The first chord is accented. This leaves the word "shall" without accent, and the music moves with a sustained, legato flow and a gradual increase from the word "how" to the word "meet" which has a decided accent.

This phrase is characterized by a relaxed, deliberate tempo which builds smoothly and with dignity to the climax with a hold on the final chord, which is decreased in volume as the chord is held. No breath should be taken during this phrase, but adequate time is given for deliberate breath after the phrase has closed and before the second phrase begins.

It is proper to linger on the next to the last chord in each phrase. This will bring about a feeling of *ritardando* at each fermata. Cadences are extremely important in this music and a luscious character can be given them by a slight lingering on the penultimate chord.

The second phrase is sung with a brighter tone and a slight increase in speed.

The third phrase is begun without a break in rhythm and is similar to the first phrase. The fourth phrase imitates the second.

The fifth phrase is sung firmly and solidly with all voices using equal strength for all notes. The sixth phrase is slightly softer, and the final phrase is sung quietly and with deep feeling, as a prayer.

We are now ready to discuss some of the problems of the voice parts, beginning with the first phrase:

"How shall I fitly meet Thee"

The altos sing the most important part in this phrase. It is not the melody, but it establishes the character of the phrase and it is of paramount importance rhythmically.

The chief vocal problem is to hold each vowel without change through all of the first tone and practically all of the second tone in each pair of eighth-notes. This same problem is met by each voice at different places in this piece. Listen carefully to retain a sustained and unvarying quality of tone while passing from the first to the second eighth-note in each pair. This is a highly profitable exercise for the attention and for the ear.

A slight stress or pulsation is felt on the first note in each pair of eighth-notes. This is produced by a slight increase in breath pressure from the diaphragm with a relaxed throat. This stress by pressure is particularly appropriate at the points of dissonance with the soprano at the beginning of each syllable on the word "fitly" and on the word "meet."

The word "meet" is accented by all voices, but although the soprano and bass diminish throughout the time-value of the chord, the alto sings its eighth-notes without decrease in volume and then diminishes on the final word, "Thee." Alto and tenor should fit their parts together on the word "meet," bringing out their respective eighth-notes, A, $G\sharp$, B, A.

Sopranos must not sing too loud on this phrase. They should avoid an accent on the word "shall." An absolute legato is maintained except when moving from tones F to E on the word "fitly." This word makes a perfect legato impossible because the t intercepts the flow of tone. The t will be sung distinctly and quickly in order to reduce the length of interruption of the singing tone. The accent on the word "meet" will be very positive with a long sustained vowel sound and a quick pronunciation of the *t*, leading into the final word, "Thee," which should be well tapered off.   This final chord requires a rather dark quality.

Tenors will find their first difficulty on the second eighth-note of the syllable "fit."   As the tenors ascend to the note *D*, they will give increased breath pressure to assure definite, positive tone on this top note.   Do not hurry over the eighth-notes.   Each receives a beat. On the word "meet," accent the first eighth-note, sing the *G♯* distinctly, and diminish on the final quarter-notes *A* and *G♯*.

The bass has a general *crescendo* from the first tone to the note *C* at the top of the scale passage.   Maintain full value for each note with particular attention to the eighth-notes and the quarter-note *C*, which must be given full duration.   There must be a strong accent on the note *F* of the word "meet," with a *diminuendo* to match the soprano.

"And give Thee welcome due"

Basses now have an opportunity to demonstrate that they can sing paired eighth-notes with distinctness and purity of vowel sound. Accent the word "give," and sing the following eighth-notes firmly and prominently, with a deep, resonant, dignified tone.   Observe the comments on the alto part in the previous phrase.

Sopranos will require increased breath pressure on the two sixteenth-notes* in order to maintain the basic *ay* sound.   Sing these notes deliberately and firmly, and do not permit the *l* to appear until after the note *D* is established.

Tenors will build up to a firm accent on the beginning of the word "welcome."

All voices will feel an accent on the final chord.   In the compound vowel sound for the word "due," the *ee* must be pronounced distinctly and quickly, the *oo* being held for the full value with a slight *diminuendo*.   There is no break in the rhythm at the end of this phrase.

"The nations long to greet Thee"

Again the altos have the chief problem of singing paired notes without change of vowel sound.

Sing this in the same style as the first phrase, but with dramatic significance to the word "long."   This is accomplished by holding the liquid *l* and moving from it to the vowel sound with a restrained, explosive impulse.

"And I would greet Thee too"

The basses now sing the paired eighth-notes with pure vowel sound.   This phrase is sung in the style of the second phrase.   It is

* or semiquavers

brighter, more hopeful, and taken at a freshened pace in contrast to the previous phrase which is more sadly dramatic.

"O Fount of light, shine brightly"

Here the tenors have their best opportunity to sing paired tones on a single vowel sound. Their success in maintaining an unchanging vowel sound on each pair of notes will have much to do with beauty of this phrase.

Observe the comma for a half breath. Tenors and basses must sing the second eighth-note on the word "light" before taking this breath. Sopranos and altos will sustain the quarter-note until the tenors and basses have sung both of the eighth-notes so that all voices may breathe together. This quick breath will be taken through the mouth, of course. This is a powerful phrase, and a firm accent is given to the word "brightly."

The fermata is sustained solidly and with power to its end without *diminuendo*.

"Upon my darkened heart"

This entire phrase is very dark in color. There must be great humility expressed in the words "darkened heart." The tenors predominate throughout the phrase, singing with a resonant tone. On the final eighth-notes, the tenors will sound like 'cellos. These notes are sung lovingly with a slight retard and a delayed approach to the final chord. It may be necessary for the other voices to border on a hum in order to permit the tenor to stand out with sufficient prominence.

The altos will use a broad chest quality on the eighth-notes and will sing the final *C#* of the cadence boldly so that it will be heard above the other notes of the chord.

"That I may serve Thee rightly"

At "I may" the soprano and tenor, moving in tenths (octave and three degrees apart), must stand out. On "serve Thee," the alto and tenor move together and occupy an equally prominent position.

The bass voice is featured throughout this phrase. On the word "I" the note should be sustained as long as possible. *G* is to be held for its full value. Be sure to sing *F#* on the word "may."

"And know Thee as Thou art"

This phrase is the most legato of all. It must be sung quietly and with deep suppressed feeling. The final measure must be handled with particular care. In this measure the first two notes may each have a slight emphasis in the form of a very gently feminine swell, with the last chord sung truly *pianissimo*.

HOW SHALL I FITLY MEET THEE

Chorale from the *Christmas Oratorio* (1734)

PAUL GERHARDT (1607-1676)
Trans by the Rev. J. Troutbeck
Edited by John Smallman

Melody by
HANS LEO HASSLER (1564-1612)
Harmonized by Johann Sebastian Bach
(1685-1750)

77384-117

pp ⌢   *mf*

greet   Thee,   And   I   would   greet ____ Thee
gree - - (t) thee   ah - (nd) ah - (ee) woo - (d) gree - (t) thee
ee   ee   ah   ah   oh   ee   ee

pp ⌢   *mf*

greet _____ Thee,   And   I   would   greet   Thee
gree - - (t) thee   ah - (nd) ah - (ee) woo - (d) gree - (t) thee
ee   ee   ah   ah   oh   ee   ee

pp ⌢   *mf*

greet _____ Thee,   And   I ____ would   greet   Thee__
gree - - (t) thee   ah - (nd) ah - (ee) woo - (d) gree - (t) thee__
ee   ee   ah   ah   oh   ee   ee

pp ⌢   *mf*

greet   Thee,   And   I   would   greet ____ Thee
gree - - (t) thee   ah - (nd) ah - (ee) woo - (d) gree - (t) thee
ee   ee   ah   ah   oh   ee   ee

pp ⌢   *mf*

f   ⌢   *mp*

too.   O   Fount ___ of   light,   shine   bright -   ly   Up -
too   oh   fah - (oont) aw - (v) lah - (eet) shah - (een) brah - (eet) lee   uh - (p)
oh   oh   ah   oh   ah   ah   ah   ee   ah

f   ⌢   *mp*

too.   O ___ Fount   of ___ light,   shine   bright -   ly   Up -
too   oh ___ fah - (oont) aw - (v) lah - (eet) shah - (een) brah - (eet) lee   uh - (p)
oh   oh   ah   oh   ah   ah   ah   ee   ah

f   ⌢   *mp*

too.   O   Fount   of   light,   shine   bright -   ly   Up -
too   oh   fah - (oont) aw - (v) lah - (eet) shah - (een) brah - (eet) lee   uh - (p)
oh   oh   ah   oh   ah   ah   ah   ee   ah

f   ⌢   *mp*

too.   O   Fount   of   light,   shine   bright -   ly   Up -
too   oh   fah - (oont) aw - (v) lah - (eet) shah - (een) brah - (eet) lee   uh - (p)
oh   oh   ah   oh   ah   ah   ah   ee   ah

f   ⌢   *mp*

Chapter XII

SEVERAL TONES ON ONE VOWEL SOUND

In These Delightful, Pleasant Groves—Henry Purcell (1658-1695)

WE NOW approach the interesting task of singing several tones in a scale passage on one vowel sound. One of the essential points is to sing all of the tones without change of vowel quality. This will be rather easy in the following piece, because the word is "laugh" which has the simple vowel sound *ah*, and the aspirate *f* has no pitch and does not appear until the end of the scale passage. Another vowel sound which appears in a scale passage is the *eh* sound in "revels." This is a simple vowel sound and the *v* does not appear until the end of the scale passage. The altos have several tones in the form of a shake on the word "cheer." This is more difficult because the *r* must not be permitted to intrude before its time.

But there is another point in regard to scale singing on a single vowel. There is danger of sliding from one tone to another in a semi-*glissando* style, without clearly defining the pitch of each note in the scale. Besides being slovenly, this habit destroys the character of the part and does not permit it to stand out as a self-respecting voice part. Consequently, it is necessary to devote particular attention to detaching the tones of a scale-wise passage slightly, in order to avoid the dangers of the *glissando*, and to give character and distinction to the scale-wise passage. Ordinarily in a chorus, a scale passage sounds less detached than the individual singers seem to be singing. Because of this it is safe to exaggerate the idea of detaching the tones in a scale passage, rather than to lean too much toward the idea of slurring scales.

This piece has some difficulties of pronunciation previous to the scale passage. The words "let us" appear on fast moving eighth-notes which require a free and nimble tongue. The whole piece moves quite rapidly and requires the most clean-cut and accurate pronunciation.

There are several interesting examples of different vowel qualities, based on the same basic vocal position. For example, *ah* is the basic vocal position for the word "our," which has a very broad sound. *Ah* is also the basic vocal position for the first vowel sound in "happy," a very thin tone. The vowel sound in "laugh" is midway between the two. Although these three vowel sounds are all different, they are basically related to the vocal position *ah*.

At the beginning of this composition, we have two phrases of three measures each. Retain the feeling of the three-measure phrases by keeping rather strict time. In the third measure, there is a chord for a half-note, followed by a rest of a quarter duration,—no more. The same is true in the sixth measure.

The three half-notes which appear on the words "pleasant groves" must be sung firmly and with full value. Especially the word "groves" must be sung for a full half-note value, the *vz* not appearing until the third quarter-note in the measure. In some cases it will seem wise to give a little push to the second quarter-note value in this half-note on the word "groves." This is particularly useful in measure 6, where the first sopranos have the *F♯*.

In addition to the word "groves," there are certain other words which appear on half-note chords and require a slight pressure of the breath to swell them out to full value. The word "loves" in measures 11 and 22, is one of these. The word "dance" in measures 24 and 26 is treated with a slight pressure. The half-notes in measures 32, 33 and 34 are sung very boldly and firmly. The breath pushes these chords out, slightly exaggerating their length. The *s* sound of the word "thus" does not appear until the vowel has sounded a full half-note.

Staccato marks are placed above the last two syllables of the word "delightful." The *t* which is between these syllables tends to separate them but the *l* sound which introduces one of the syllables and closes the other one is too liquid in quality to permit a true *staccato*. A recognition of the musical effect indicated by the two *staccato* marks on this word will help the singer to approximate the effect indicated.

The final syllable of "delightful" is given the phonetic spelling "fuhl," with a basic *oh* position. Some voices may give a more accurate and resonant pronunciation if they think the syllable *ah*. The pronunciation of *uh* falls between these basic positions and the side from which it is approached will be determined by the individual voices. A similar situation with the *uh* sound in the word "welcome" was discussed in the previous chapter.

The word "celebrate" must be sung buoyantly and with much spirit so that each syllable pops out with a little accent of its own. As this word is sung six times, it is possible to study it carefully, enunciating it identically on each repetition.

There are only twenty-five words used in the text, but some of these are repeated several times. This makes it even more essential to study them carefully. "In," "happy," and "let us celebrate" appear six times; "pipe" and "these delightful groves" appear four times; "thus" is heard three times; and "love," "danger," "spring," "revels," and "cheerful" appear twice in prominent places. If the accurate pronunciation of these important words is carefully studied before beginning to sing, it will save time in rehearsal.

In measures 10 and 21, breath is indicated to separate the repetitions of the word "happy," but this must be a quick half-breath.

There are nine cases in which a new phrase begins on the fourth beat following a rest. These entrances must be very clean. Observe this particularly in measures 22 and 24.

Detach the words "laugh" and "and" in measure 31, pressing each firmly to give it prominence and make an *allargando* with strong pressure on the word "sing" in measure 32. It may be necessary to take breath before the final "laugh and sing" in order to end this passage with vigor and firmness.

In measures 27-31, the soprano and bass sing the same melodic outline except that they are an octave and three degrees (a tenth) apart. Practice these two parts together until they balance each other and maintain accurate intonation with each other. Likewise, alto and tenor in measures 27-30 are paired and should be practiced together.

Reserve the *f* sound in the word "laugh" until the full value of the final quarter has been expended on the *ah* vowel sound. This really places the *f* on the rest except in measures 30-31, where there are no rests.

"Sing" in measure 32 and "thus" in measure 33 are written as half-notes but they may be treated as dotted half-notes with the final consonant on the last quarter of the measure.

When the word "revels" begins on the third beat in measure 37, accent the third beat but do not accent the beginning of the following measure. What a glorious opportunity for pure vocal tone on these quarter-note runs! Each voice should vie with its associates in producing a pure tone and accurate intonation with no sliding between tones.

In measure 42, start the new passage on "revels" as though it were a distant echo of measure 37. Do not permit a slackening of the tempo at this point.

Sing the quarter-note scale passage, beginning with measure 27, in a semi-detached manner. In measures 39, 40, 44 and 45, altos should detach the eighth-notes, shaking them out like laughter. In the final chord, the tenor will sing B♮ very accurately in tune in order to bring out the character of the major chord.

Although the metronome mark is given as 82, some choruses will prefer to sing it slower in order to give every tone and chord its necessary distinctness and resonance. A few very excellent choruses may choose a quicker pace. Accuracy and style are more important than speed.

IN THESE DELIGHTFUL, PLEASANT GROVES
(1676)

Edited by John Smallman

HENRY PURCELL (1658-1695)

System 1:

cel - e - brate, let us cel - e - brate our hap - py, hap - py loves; In
seh-(l)ee-bray-(eet) leh-(t) uh- (s)seh-(l)ee-bray-(eet) ah-(oor)hah-pee hah-pee luh-(vz) ih-(n)
ay ee ay ay ah ay ee ay ah ah ee ah ee ah ee

cel - e - brate, let us cel - e - brate our hap - py, hap - py loves; In
seh-(l)ee-bray-(eet) leh-(t) uh- (s)seh-(l)ee-bray-(eet) ah-(oor)hah-pee hah-pee luh-(vz) ih-(n)
ay ee ay ay ah ay ee ay ah ah ee ah ee ah ee

cel - e - brate, let us cel - e - brate our hap - py, hap - py loves; In
seh-(l)ee-bray-(eet) leh-(t) uh- (s)seh-(l)ee-bray-(eet) ah-(oor)hah-pee hah-pee luh-(vz) ih-(n)
ay ee ay ay ah ay ee ay ah ah ee ah ee ah ee

cel - e - brate, let us cel - e - brate our hap - py, hap - py loves; In
seh-(l)ee-bray-(eet) leh-(t) uh- (s)seh-(l)ee-bray-(eet) ah-(oor)hah-pee hah-pee luh-(vz) ih-(n)
ay ee ay ay ah ay ee ay ah ah ee ah ee ah ee

System 2:

these de - light - ful, pleas - ant groves, In these de - light - ful,
thee-(z)dee-lah-(eet)fuh- (l)pleh-(z)ah-(nt)groh-(vz) ih-(n)thee-(z)dee-lah-(eet)fuh-(l)
ee ee ah oh ay ah oh ee ee ee ah oh

these de - light - ful, pleas - ant groves, In these de - light - ful,
thee-(z)dee-lah-(eet)fuh- (l)pleh-(z)ah-(nt)groh-(vz) ih-(n)thee-(z)dee-lah-(eet)fuh-(l)
ee ee ah oh ay ah oh ee ee ee ah oh

these de - light - ful, pleas - ant groves, In these de - light - ful,
thee-(z)dee-lah-(eet)fuh- (l)pleh-(z)ah-(nt)groh-(vz) ih-(n)thee-(z)dee-lah-(eet)fuh-(l)
ee ee ah oh ay ah oh ee ee ee ah oh

these de - light - ful, pleas - ant groves, In these de - light - ful,
thee-(z)dee-lah-(eet)fuh- (l)pleh-(z)ah-(nt)groh-(vz) ih-(n)thee-(z)dee-lah-(eet)fuh-(l)
ee ee ah oh ay ah oh ee ee ee ah oh

p
mf
25
loves: Let's pipe, pipe and dance, let's pipe, pipe and
luh - (vz) leh - (ts) pah-(eep) pah-(eep) ah-(nd) dah - (ns) leh - (ts) pah-(eep) pah-(eep) ah-(nd)
ah ay ah ah ah ah ay ah ah ah
f
dance, dance and laugh, laugh, laugh,
dah-(ns) dah-(ns) ah - (nd) lah - (f) lah - (f) lah -
ah ah ah ah ah ah
dance, laugh, laugh, laugh, laugh
dah-(ns) lah - (f) lah - (f) lah - (f) lah -
ah ah ah ah ah
dah - (ns) lah - (f) lah - (f) lah - (f) lah -
dah-(ns) dah (ns) ah - (nd) lah - (f) lah - (f) lah -

CHAPTER XIII

TUNING SUSTAINED CHORDS

Adoramus Te, Christe—Giovanni P. da Palestrina (1514?-1594)

GOOD intonation is the production of music with all parts in tune. It means that every voice must move exactly the correct distance in pitch when progressing from one tone to another. This will make every chord sound in tune with itself and the piece will end without any sharping or flatting from the pitch at which it was started.

In developing good intonation, proper attention must be given to good chording. Take time to listen to sustained chords and judge whether your voice is fitting into the chord smoothly. If a chord is well tuned it will sound smooth. If it is out of tune, there will be a roughness in the chord.

Many chords contain only three tones. When a quartet is singing, one of the tones of the chord must be duplicated in two voice parts. This duplication may occur at the unison or at the octave. These two intervals are the easiest intervals to sing in tune, and the simplest for the ear to understand and adjust accurately.

In this number octaves are very prominent and they should be tuned in every chord. They appear between every possible pair of voices. In the first measure, *D* is held by the soprano and the bass. In measure 2, the tenor and bass have an octave on *A*. Measure 3 has an octave *D* between soprano and alto which is followed in the next measure by an octave *A* between bass and tenor. In measure 5, the alto and bass hold the *D*, while measure 6 gives the *D* to soprano and alto. The final measure of the phrase gives the octave to bass and tenor.

Obviously, this phrase cannot descend far from the correct pitch, if the two tones *A* and *D* with their octaves are held perfectly in tune. This is not difficult when sufficient attention is given to this point, because *D* is the key tone and *A* is the fifth degree of the scale. Establish a feeling of tonality with *D* as the key tone and *A* as the next most prominent tone of the scale, and then tune these tones and their octaves to form a basis for the intonation of the first phrase.

Each phrase should be studied, every singer drawing a line between the two tones in each chord which produce an octave. Pencil marks between the tones which produce an octave will help to direct the attention toward tuning these tones. As a beginning exercise it is sometimes helpful to sing octaves on various tones, using each of the four basic vowel sounds, and making all possible combinations, such as bass and tenor, bass and alto, tenor and soprano, alto and soprano, bass and soprano, alto and tenor.

The first chorus for this number should include one-third to one-half the number of voices assigned to the second chorus part. The two choruses are combined at the climax of the composition. This must be accomplished with a feeling of gradual increase in sound and without the idea of additional voices being added suddenly. The climax must be built gradually and smoothly. A slight *allargando* is effective, starting three measures before the place the two choirs join and continuing for three measures after they have joined.

Devote particular attention to the cadences. There is a *ritardando* marked for the cadences at the ends of each of the first four phrases. This makes it possible to bring out the moving part found in the tenor of measures 6, 20 and 26, and the alto of measure 13.

Measures 7 and 21 will be drawn out with the *ritard.*, the second chorus following immediately without any break.

The whole number is based on rather a sombre tone color and it must be sung without any feeling of restlessness or hurry. Sing it deliberately and smoothly with every attention to chording as if each member of the chorus loved every chord.

The Latin text may be translated as follows:

> *Adoramus te, Christe!*
> We adore Thee, O Christ!
>
> *et benedicimus tibi.*
> and we bless Thee.
>
> *Quia per sanctam crucem tuam*
> Because, through Thy holy cross
>
> *redemisti mundum,*
> Thou has redeemed the world,
>
> *qui passus es pro nobis, Domine,*
> Thou who has suffered for us, O Lord,
>
> *miserere nobis!*
> have mercy on us!

This composition is commonly printed in the key of A-minor with the chords in close position. We are using D-minor with open chords because it is easier to hear and to tune the octaves and fifths when they are open and have no intervening voices. Thus it gives a singularly obvious and clear-cut opportunity to experiment with the principles laid down in this chapter. Also, this arrangement gives an artistically ethereal effect which is lost when the chords are compressed. To secure the best results, the soprano must be extremely light and the alto must be rather heavy. Second sopranos can combine with the altos, leaving only the lightest sopranos on the top part. Altos, tenors, and basses will balance their chords carefully, bringing into prominence whichever tone is needed to give the proper color to the harmonies, or to illuminate a melodic bit.

ADORAMUS TE

Antiphonal
Motet for Mixed Voices

Edited by John Smallman

GIOVANNI P. DA PALESTRINA
(1514-1594)

77384-117

Chorus I
p a tempo
30
dim.
Qui - a per san - ctam cru - cem tu - - am re -
kwee - ah peh - (r) sah-(nk) tah - (m) kroo - tcheh - (m) too - - ah - (m) reh -
ee ah ay ah ah oh ay oh ah ay
a tempo
p
Chorus II
35
pp
mf
- de - mi - sti mun - - dum, qui pas - sus es
- day - mee - (s) tee moo - - (n) doo - (m) kwee pah - soo - (s) eh - (s)
ay ee ee oh oh ee ah oh ay

CHAPTER XIV

TUNING BY PITCH IMITATION

The Silver Swan—Orlando Gibbons (1583-1625)

This is the best known of many excellect madrigals written during the seventeenth century. Its beauties are many and numerous but it includes many difficulties.

The text is worthy of serious study without the music. Its six lines are beautiful to hear when recited by a person with a well modulated voice and a heart which responds to beauty. The twenty-one measures of music (seven of them repetition) are an appropriate setting for this little gem of poetry.

This number requires balance between the parts and delicacy of blend. Balance must be judged from the stand-point of the prominence of certain tones of the chord, considered vertically, and the prominence of certain melodic lines, considered horizontally.

To judge the balance of a chord it is considered by itself as a stationary blend of superimposed tones. In some chords every tone must be equally prominent. In other chords there may be certain tones which should be subordinated or a tone which must be sung more prominently than the other tones of the chord.

Melodically and contrapuntally the attention is horizontal and the interest is constantly moving as it flows along the line of melody. Usually, the voice part moving along the tones of a melody is of more importance than the other voices sustained on the long tones of a chord. When all the voice parts are melodic in character, the problem deepens and we must decide which are the most important melodies before we will know which voice will be the most prominent.

Blend is determined largely by pronunciation and intonation. The pronunciation is indicated accurately in the text. Intonation will require the constant service of the ear. This music calls for intense mental concentration. Every singer must be on his toes mentally and there should be no distractions.

Whenever two voice parts have the same tone at a unison or an octave, they should tune carefully. On the very first chord, the second sopranos and altos have a unison which must make a perfect blend. The first sopranos, being an octave higher, will tune exactly to the low *C* as though their tone were an emanation from the lower tone.

The second chord is identical with the first, except that the second soprano moves to a tone which she tunes with the bass, an octave lower. In the third chord, the first soprano and bass both hold *D* which they should tune accurately. In the beginning of the second measure, the first and second sopranos tune *E* carefully, while the alto and bass observe the resonant effect they produce by the perfect octave they sustain.

It is unnecessary to list all of these places for tuning unisons and octaves. They occur in every measure and the singers must be alert to utilize these opportunities for testing the intonation and the perfect blend of parts.

From the horizontal or contrapuntal standpoint, we must give prominence to significant melodies in individual parts. This is especially important when one voice imitates another. In such case, the imitating voices are given prominence while the other voices sing more softly as a part of the background. Starting with the fourth beat of measure three, the second soprano has a melody which carries through 4 beats, covering a scale-wise passage, from *C* up to *G*, with a quarter-note on the final *G*, a dotted quarter on the first *C* and three intervening eighth-notes. The first *C*, being a long tone equivalent to a tied quarter and eighth, and introducing an important melody, is sung very firmly. The eighth-notes are somewhat detached in order to give them prominence. The second soprano sets the character for this melody, but she has no more than started it when the bass begins to imitate her, starting on the first beat of measure 4. The tenor follows immediately, starting on the second beat of measure 4. These three voices occupy the center of the stage in measure 4 and it would be well for them to rehearse this measure alone a few times. The composer has done his part toward shifting the first soprano and alto into the background by giving them sustained tones in the low part of their range. The first sopranos and altos must assist in accomplishing the purpose of the composer by singing their sustained tones, at the beginning of measure 4, rather softly and subordinating their parts to the more interesting moving parts of the other three voices. If the soprano and alto sustain a perfect *oh* vowel sound, it will form the proper background for the changing vowels of the three flowing parts.

When the second soprano starts her melody on the last beat of measure 3, she sets the pitch which will be imitated an octave lower on the first beat of the 4th measure by the bass. On the second beat of this measure, the tenors enter on exactly the same pitch used by the basses.

Although these solos necessitate accurate imitation in style, they also demand accurate imitation in pitch. Attention to this detail will assist greatly in establishing perfect intonation.

On the fourth beat of measure 4, the first soprano starts a four-note melody which is followed one beat later by the bass. This is difficult because the bass is two octaves below the voice it is imitating and the words are different. But if these two parts are rehearsed separately on this four note unit, the intonation can be checked accurately. It is interesting to observe in measure 5 that the three inner voices can be easily subordinated. The second soprano is singing a harmonic part with the bass. The alto is singing tones which can be easily subordinated and the tenor has very little movement to distract the attention.

In measure 7, starting with the second beat, the basses have a four-note descending fragment which is imitated two octaves higher by the first soprano. These two parts can well be rehearsed alone until their relation is perfectly apparent to the ear. The alto imitates the bass five tones higher, beginning on the last beat of measure 7. This is an important relationship, and the basses and altos should rehearse together until their pitch relationship is thoroughly understood.

The tenor in measure 10 takes a six-note melody which is imitated at the beginning of the following measure by the bass five tones lower. Again rehearse these two parts alone until the pitch relationship is perfectly clear. The alto in measure 11 sings "thus sung" on the tones G and C which are imitated three beats later by the soprano an octave higher.

These points of imitational singing deserve to be carefully studied until they are thoroughly understood by the ear and can be sung with great nicety of pitch discrimination in order to hold the music in tune.

Returning now to the beginning for additional suggestions, observe the beginning is marked p. This does not mean a lifeless tone. The voices must be concentrated and properly placed in order to make the tone spin. Notice the *uh* sound in "the" is based on *ah*, but the *uh* sound in silver is based on *oh*. Give particular attention to the balance between the parts. Swell slightly to the word "swan" which is marked *mp*. This word must be sung with significance. First sopranos, altos and basses give a slight swell without obscuring the second sopranos and tenors which are the more important parts. The alto will require a deep, firm chest tone on these two measures.

The comma after the word "swan" is really a point of expression for the second soprano, because it gives her opportunity to introduce the words "who living" with more implied meaning. These words are repeated with additional signficance by the first soprano, alto and bass as they enter the third measure. These voices will give a slight stress to the first syllable of the word "living," making it a vibrant tone.

The tenors will increase in volume as they ascend the scale passage in measure 3, and the other voices gradually subordinate themselves. The tenors must sing the eighth-notes of their scale passage slightly detached. The word "note" as sung by the first sopranos and altos will be soft and sad in quality.

Although the word "death" is sung with meaning by all voices, the first sopranos are particularly cautioned to observe this point. They will give dramatic significance to the word by exaggerating the D effect. With this stress on the consonant, the throat must be kept open in order to assist in giving the air of mystery and awe which should permeate "when death approached."

The word "unlocked" is accented on the second syllable always. This is quite as true for the bass in measure 5 as for the alto, tenor and first soprano, when they sing the word together as they move into measure 6. "Silent" will be accented firmly on the first syllable. The cadence, ending on the word "throat" is sung quietly and with true falling inflection. Time is taken to treat this word with deliberation, as it ends a cadence, before the next phrase is begun.

"Leaning" is sung with a considerable stress on the l. Think the l. The tone should carry forward without decrease as though the singer were leaning against the tone. The voices must be very smooth and even. This legato effect is aided by the n in the middle of the word "leaning," which must sing straight through from its beginning to its end without any relaxation of pressure on its spinning tone.

There is a slight relaxation in the second sopranos and basses as they close the phrase on the words "her breast," but when the first soprano sings this phrase in measures 8 and 9, she must maintain the breath pressure in coming down the phrase. The basses and second sopranos must be very careful of their pitch and balance in measure 7. The second sopranos and tenors in measure 8 will sing the eighth-notes somewhat detached. The r of "reedy" should be rolled.

In measures 9, 10 and 11, the words "reedy" and "shore" are stressed. The r of "shore" should be reduced to the vanishing point for the sake of tone quality. This is particularly true in the first soprano part which is building up through measure 10 into measure 11.

The words "thus sung" are to be uttered deliberately with each note somewhat stressed, although the principal accent must be obviously on the words "sung," "first," and "last." The words "thus" and "sung" will need to be somewhat detached because of the connected s sounds. Otherwise, the effect might be more like Chinese than English. The first soprano from the fourth beat of measure 11 to the first beat of measure 13, will press each tone by the breath and will almost detach them in order to avoid any suspicion of sliding from one tone to another. This will tend to slow the pace, and will bring the tempo down to that of the first six measures, if there has been a slight increase starting in measure 7.

All vowel sounds of "thus sung her first" are written phonetically as *uh* but the first two are based on *ah* and the last two are based on *oh*.

In the alto and bass the *E♭* of the 12th measure is important. The tenor will give emotional significance by pressure with vibrant quality to the last tone in measure 12, which is followed by the falling scale in the cadence. The cadence is finished very quietly and smoothly to measure 14.

The word "farewell" must be charged with beautiful quality. Sing it with an open throat but very softly and with intense feeling. The altos will strive for quality in measure 15, in order to make their tones felt. In the final measures, the following words are stressed: "close," "eyes," "geese," "swans," "live," and "fools."

In the next to the last measure, the basses sing the word "fools" firmly but softly. The sopranos stress the word "fools" when it makes its final appearance in measure 20. The other voices take a deliberate breath after the first beat of the measure, leaving the bass sounding alone. After a slight pause, they continue with their cadence which must be very soft with unified pronunciation and perfect intonation.

THE SILVER SWAN

Canzonet for Five Voices (1612)

Edited by J. S. and E. H. W.

ORLANDO GIBBONS (1583-162

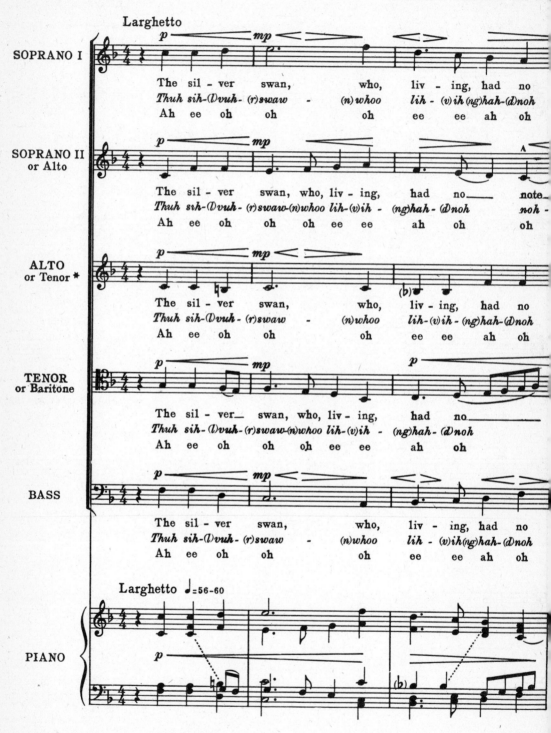

* Tenors will read this part an octave higher.

77384-117

* In measures 5-7 some of the Alto and Tenor notes have been interchanged to relieve the Altos of a few low notes.

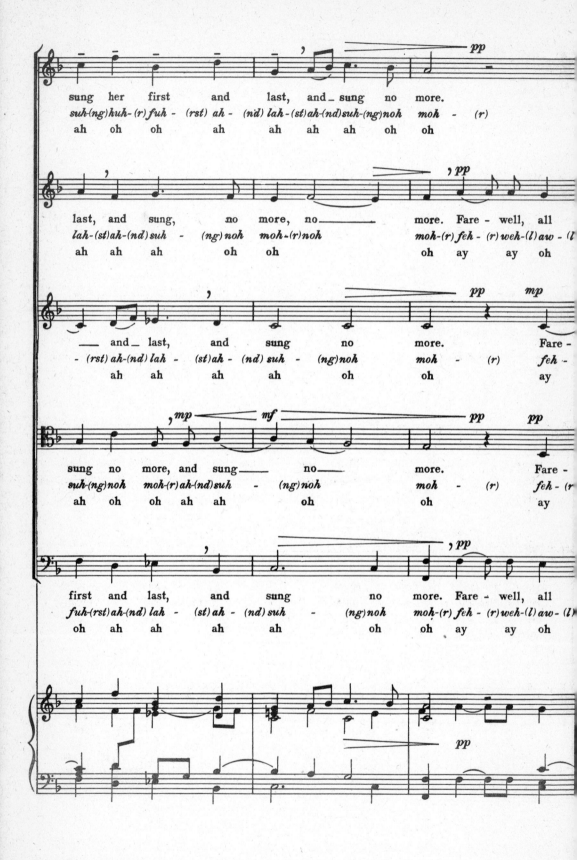

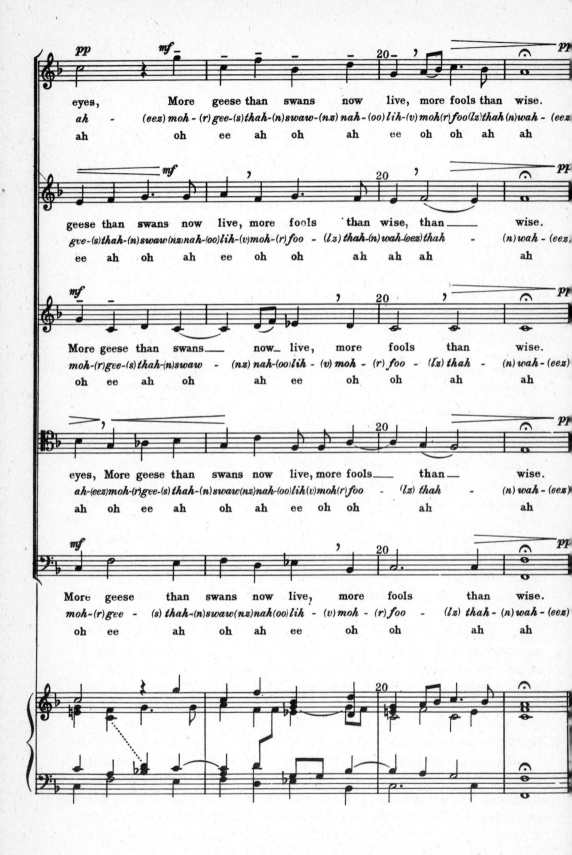

Chapter XV

AGOGIC ACCENT

Lo, How a Rose e'er Blooming—Michael Praetorius (1571-1621)

Accents play an important part in giving character to music. In speech we recognize two types of accent. One is dynamic, consisting of forceful and, oftentimes, abrupt utterances, as when we shout, "fire fire, fire!" This type of accent usually suggests excitement, gaity, or strength. Consequently, it predominates in music dealing with the dance, rejoicing, or power. Splendid use of this will be noted in *In These Delightful*, *Pleasant Groves*, *Now is the Month of Maying*, and *Lovely Lady*.

The second type of accent occurs in speech when we sustain a word, drawing out its sound for a longer duration than it would normally have, in order to direct attention to that word. This is known as the agogic accent. It occurs in speech in words which are charged with emotion and feeling. Words of tenderness, affection, or beauty are often fondled and stroked by the voice as they are pronounced. The stage lover says, "I love you," stretching the word "love" as though he regretted to part with it. In music the long tones or chords contain the agogic accent. In perfect compositions the most important words will be sung on the longest tones so that the agogic accent of music will stress the most important points of the text.

Lo, How a Rose e'er Blooming consists almost entirely of half-notes and quarter-notes, the alto being the only voice having notes of any other time-value. Therefore the half-notes attract the agogic accent and the quarter-notes are not stressed. In the first phrase, which consists of two and one-half measures, there are agogic accents on "Lo" and both syllables of "blooming." There are no important accents on "how a rose e'er." The word "rose" will attract a slight accent because of its significance, but when this phrase is properly molded from the musical standpoint, the three half-notes will be sustained for the full value, creating distinct agogic accents, while the intervening quarter-notes are sung smoothly and tranquilly without stress or accent of any type.

In the second phrase, which begins with the third beat of measure 3 and continues to the end of measure 5, the soprano will accent the half-notes, treating the two tied quarter-notes as a half-note so that the tones *C*, *A* and *G* have agogic accents. The *A* and *G* in measure 4 have slight dynamic accents, also. The bass has four half-notes in

73

this phrase, each of which receives an agogic accent. The tenor must treat the two tied quarter-notes as a half-note, giving an agogic accent to the tone *B* which is sustained firmly into the 5th measure, resolving into *A* on the second beat. The alto has a long tone in measure 4. It is interesting to notice that the text of the second verse fits this alto part much better than the first verse. In the second verse the length of the tones in the alto brings a natural stress to the words "rose" and "mind." In each case the alto will have difficulty in making the eighth-note effective.

Attention to the natural stress which belongs to long chords will give depth and meaning to music of this type. Dwelling on long chords which are nicely balanced and well in tune, is one of the delights of choral singing.

This charming piece consists of seventeen measures—a five-measure period which is repeated, followed by a short two-measure interlude, returning again at the end to a five-measure period which is very similar to the first period. The chief variation in the fina period occurs on the word "winter" when the tenor moves from *A* to *G♯*, producing a major triad in contrast to the minor triad of the first period when the tenor moves from *A* to *G♮*. This distinction must be brought out clearly by the tenor and recognized thoroughly by all voices. When the minor triad is used with *G♮* in the tenor, it is well to treat this minor triad rather tenderly and gently, shaping it off to end the phrase gracefully. But when the *G♯* is used, the chord may be taken more resolutely and firmly, as befits the bright major triad.

There is an indication to breathe in the middle of measure 3, although some choruses prefer to sing the entire first period of five measures without taking breath. The word "Lo" can be treated with a very slight swell, and a half breath can be taken after it, if desired. The *ritard.* must be gentle and not excessive. The final chord on the word "sprung" must be given opportunity to sound firmly before the *diminuendo* carries it to *pp*.

The contrasting section in measure 11 and 12 is intended to be sung brightly and somewhat *marcato*. The alto will be careful to sing *E♮* on the word "came," and she will detach the three notes on the word "bright," taking care to use the unchanged vowel sound *ah* on these three notes. The soprano should hold the low *D* firmly for full two beats, while the alto is singing these tones. The word "cold" can be sung with strong consonants in order to give the effect of cold. In the word "winter," a strong *n* sound can be introduced. The final phrase must be sung very tenderly.

The whole piece provides a good example of smooth singing with gentle, sustained agogic accent except in measures 11 and 12, and slightly in measures 13 and 14.

If the composer had attempted to make the agogic accent correspond with the metric accent he might have used the following notation:

No matter what notation is used, the music will be sung with
the rhythmic swing determined by the relationship of long and short
notes, the melodic contour, and the words. Of these various factors
the agogic accent is of greatest importance in determining the rhythm
for a piece of this type. Sing this number smoothly, and enjoy its
gently sustained long chords.

LO, HOW A ROSE E'ER BLOOMING

English version by Dr. Theodore Baker*
Edited by E.H.W.

16th Century Melody
Harmonized by Michael Praetorius (1571-1621)

77384-117

rit.
pp mp a tempo
Rose I have in mind, With Ma - ry
roh - (z)ah - (ee)hah - - (v)ih - (n)mah - (eend) wih - (th) may - (ee) ree
oh ah ah ee ah ee ay ee
Rose I have in mind, With Ma - ry
roh - - (z)ah - (ee)hah - (v)ih - (n)mah - (eend) wih - (th) may - (ee) ree
oh ah ah ee ah ee ay ee
Rose I have in mind, With Ma - ry
roh - (z)ah - (ee)hah - - (v)ih - (n)mah - (eend) wih - (th) may - (ee) ree
oh ah ah ee ah ee ay ee
Rose I have in mind, With Ma - ry
roh - (z)ah - (ee)hah - - (v)ih - (n)mah - (eend) wih - (th) may - (ee) ree
oh ah ah ee ah ee ay ee
a tempo
pp mp
mf 25
we be - hold it, The Vir - gin Moth - er kind.
wee bee - hoh - (ld) ih - (t) thuh vuh - (r) jih - (n) muh - thuh - (r) kah - (eend)
ee ee oh ee ah oh ee ah ah ah
we be - hold it, The Vir - gin Moth - er kind.
wee bee - hoh - (ld) ih - (t) thuh vuh - (r) jih - (n) muh - thuh - (r) kah - (eend)
ee ee oh ee ah oh ee ah ah ah
we be - hold it, The Vir - gin Moth - er kind.
wee bee - hoh - (ld) ih - (t) thuh vuh - (r) jih - (n) muh - - thuh - (r) kah - (eend)
ee ee oh ee ah oh ee ah ah ah
we be - hold it, The Vir - gin Moth - er kind.
wee bee - hoh - (ld) ih - (t) thuh vuh - (r) jih - (n) muh - thuh - (r) kah - (eend)
ee ee oh ee ah oh ee ah ah ah
25
mf
pp

To show God's love a - right She bore to
too shoh gaw - (dz)luh - (v)uh - rah - - (eet) shee boh - (r)too
oh oh oh ah ah ah ee oh oh

To show God's love a - right _____ She bore to
too shoh gaw - (dz)luh - (v)uh - rah - - (eet) shee boh - (r)too
oh oh oh ah ah ah ee oh oh

To show God's love a - right She bore to
too shoh gaw - (dz)luh - (v)uh - rah - - (eet) shee boh - (r)too
oh oh oh ah ah ah ee oh oh

To show God's love a - right She bore to
too shoh gaw - (dz)luh - (v)uh - rah - - (eet) shee boh - (r)too
oh oh oh ah ah ah ee oh oh

men a Sav - ior, When half - spent was ___ the night.
meh - (n)uh say - (eev)yaw - (r)wheh - (n)hah - (f)speh - (nt)waw - (z)thuh nah - (eet)
ay ah ay oh ay ah ay oh ah ah

men a Sav - ior, When half - spent ___ was the night.
meh - (n)uh say - (eev)yaw - (r)wheh - (n)hah - (f)speh - (nt)waw - (z)thuh nah - (eet)
ay ah ay oh ay ah ay oh ah ah

men a Sav - ior, When half - spent was the night.
meh - (n)uh say - (eev)yaw - (r)wheh - (n)hah - (f)speh - (nt)waw - (z)thuh nah - (eet)
ay ah ay oh ay ah ay oh ah ah

men a Sav - ior, When half - spent was the night.
meh - (n)uh say - (eev)yaw - (r)wheh - (n)hah - (f)speh - (nt)waw - (z)thuh nah - (eet,)
av ah ay oh ay ah ay oh ah ah

CHAPTER XVI

DYNAMIC ACCENT

Now is the Month of Maying—Thomas Morley (1557-1603)

DYNAMIC accent consists of attacking a certain tone more abruptly and forcibly than its surrounding tones. The drummer accents certain strokes by hitting the drumhead more vigorously. The pianist accents certain tones by striking the piano-key for that tone with additional strength. Percussion instruments, like the drum, xylophone, banjo, and piano, are limited almost entirely to this type of attack. Voices also can use this type of attack, by letting a designated tone stand out as suddenly and abruptly louder than its fellows.

Flute players, through the use of the tongue, can start a tone abruptly at its full volume without such a sudden percussive effect. Trumpeters and horn players can start tones with a sudden attack which is explosive in character. Both the abruptness of the articulation and the strength of the suddenly released tone are factors in dynamic accent.

It is natural to give dynamic accents in certain places in the music for this chapter. It would be almost impossible to eliminate the accents in the examples given below. There is one line under those syllables which have a subordinate dynamic accent and there are two lines under those syllables which have a primary dynamic accent, with plenty of force to stress these tones.

When mer-ry lads are play-ing

A-danc-ing on the grass

The Spring clad all in glad-ness

Doth laugh at win-ter's sad-ness

The nymphs tread out the ground

Snall we play bar-ley-break

The examples given above are chosen from phrases in which the metrical rhythm (see page 82) and the rhythm of the music coincide. In such cases it is assumed the singer will produce these dynamic accents as a matter of course, without special signs in the music.

Sometimes these dynamic accents occur at less regular places in the phrase. In these cases there is often an indication in the form of an accent mark ʌ or > or *sf*.

Now is the Month of Maying is in direct contrast to *Lo, How a Rose e'er Blooming*. It is a dance founded largely on dynamic accent and strong, infectious rhythm. The text refers constantly to dancing on the grass in spring-time to celebrate the passing of winter. When the text refers to nymphs treading out "the ground," it refers to the rhythm of the dance. "Barley-break" is an old English folk-dance.

When listening to dance music, we are always conscious of a mental undercurrent of a regular, monotonous, unvarying alternation of strong and weak accents which follow one another in a constantly repeated simple pattern. This is the one, two, one, two, one, two, one, two, of a march; the left, right, left, right, left, right, left, right, of the drill-master; and the um-pah, um-pah, um-pah, um-pah of the parade band. It is the thing with which our toe moves when it taps in time with the band. We call this the metrical pattern or metrical rhythm.

Sometimes the melody jumps about with irregular rhythmic tricks of its own in contrast to this basic regular pulsation. This is the essence of jazz. It is an important feature of much of the music in this book. But for the greatest simplicity, we want the rhythm of the voice parts to correspond to the basic pulsation in each measure. That is the situation in this piece except where it is otherwise noted. Therefore, give a strong one, two, one, two, one, two, one, two, in every measure not otherwise marked. This will give the feeling of simple power and will arouse the spirit of the folk-dance.

The exuberance of this piece finds expression in the nonsense syllables which are a pure expression of the joy of song, unhampered by words. Special attention must be given to producing these nonsense syllables. The basic sound is the liquid *l* with the tip of the tongue at the base of the upper teeth. The *f* of the first syllable tends to bring the tone forward to the front of the mouth. But from that time on, through the set of syllables, the tip of the tongue is held firmly against the upper teeth at the front of the mouth except as it drops quickly to pronounce the *uh*, springing back instantly to its former position.

The final syllable on the sustained chord will be on the open *ah* sound. Certain other sustained tones which need to sound with an open sustained quality are given the syllable "lah." They are on comparatively long tones, such as dotted quarter-notes, half-notes, and dotted half-notes. Notes just before a breath are also sung with "lah."

These nonsense syllables can be very flat and uninteresting when sung as usually spelled, "fa, la, la." The chief problem is to impart the requisite life and distinction to them. This will be accomplished if they are sung as spelled in this text and in the manner described, maintaining a springing sensation in the tip of the tongue. Of course the singers must enunciate these syllables joyfully and with life to impart the necessary spontaneity.

Never permit these nonsense syllables to become stilted. They must always sound spontaneous. There is such a thing as being too proper and thereby sacrificing freshness. Sing these with abandon and in a spirit of fun.

As this piece is composed of dance rhythms and strong dynamic accents, the consonants must be given particular attention. Consonants more than vowels give spring and jump to the words. Consequently, we will rob the vowels if necessary in order to permit the consonants to punctuate the sound and give it rhythmic vitality. The articulation of these words will have much to do with the success of this number.

Give adequate stress to words on half-notes, such as "Maying," "playing," "sadness," "sound," "musing," and "refusing." On the word "fie," exaggerate the *tenuto*, holding it to the value of a half-note, going from it with a slight push or *crescendo* into the following measure.

There are really three verses with two musical periods or strains in each verse and only slight changes between the verses. The repetition of each period is in the nature of an echo, starting slightly softer than the first time through. A slight break may be made at the end of each verse, that is, just before the words "The Spring" and just before "Fie."

Those who desire guidance on the length of the final chord in each verse and the time to elapse between verses, may use the following plan. The chord at the end of each strain is written as a dotted half-note. Treat this as a half-note and a quarter-rest to close each strain, except at the ends of the verses as noted below.

At the end of the first verse on the repeat, when measure 16 is reached for the second time, sustain the chord for a full measure, rest for the value of three quarter-notes, and begin the second verse with the word "The" on the fourth quarter. This gives just one measure more than is indicated in the music.

At the end of the second verse, on the repeat, when measure 32 is reached for the second time, sustain the chord for one full measure and one quarter-note into the next measure. Rest for the remaining three quarters of a measure and the first half of the next measure. Begin the word "Fie" on the third quarter-note and sustain it for the value of a half-note, thus exaggerating the idea of *tenuto* and springing into the verse with a swell. This gives two measures more than indicated in the music.

At the end of the third verse, hold the chord for two full measures.

The breath marks appear rather close together. Many times they are found only two measures apart in this piece. It is not essential to breathe so often. If you can go four or even eight measures on one breath and thereby make an uninterrupted flow of rhythm and melody, it is a legitimate procedure, particularly in the first strain of each verse.

The first two measures contain three important words, "Now," "month," and "Maying," which should be accented accordingly. "Month" falls conveniently on the secondary accent in the measure and "Maying" is at the beginning of a measure on a primary accent. But "Now" comes just before the metrical accent and the insignificant word "is" appears on the first beat of the measure. In deference to the importance of the words, it is justifiable to slight the accent on the word "is" and give considerable accent to "Now." We may say that "Now" steals the accent from "is." The accents are then as follows: Now is the month of Maying.

In measure 6, the tenor and alto may trade C and F if it seems necessary although it is better to sing the notes as written. This applies also to measures 22 and 38.

The alto will need to be agile in measures 7, 23, and 39. The same applies to the tenor in measures 15, 31 and 47.

The word "lass" will be crisp and *staccato*. "Grass" is short and crisp also, even though it is somewhat longer than "lass." On the word "lass," the second soprano with its A♮ is responsible for giving the chord its bright major effect. The tenor has a similar responsibility in the chord on the word "grass." It is difficult for the tenor to sing this word high enough to be exactly in tune as it comes at the end of an ascending whole-tone scale of five notes. This paragraph applies also to measures 27 and 43.

NOW IS THE MONTH OF MAYING
Ballet for Five Voices*

Edited by John Smallman

THOMAS MORLEY (1557-1603)

* To obviate the necessity for two tenor parts, this number has been rearranged in the key of B♭ from the original in G.   †Vocalization of Fa, la, la.

77384-117

15
(second time)
ful - lul - lul - lul - lah. 2. The Spring clad all in
lul - lul - lul - lul - lah. 2. The Spring clad all in
lah, ful - lah. 2. The Spring clad all in
lah, ful - lul - lul - lah. 2. The Spring clad all in
thuh sprih-(ng)klah-(d) aw - (l) ih - (n)
glad - ness Doth laugh at Win - ter's sad - ness, Ful - lul -
glah - (d)neh - (s) duh - (th) lah - (f)ah - (t)wih - (n)tuh - (rz) sah - (d)neh - (s)
20

lul - lul - lul - lul - lul - lul - lah, ful-lul - lul - lul - lul lul lah.

lul - lul-lul - lul - lah, ful-lul-lah, ful-lul - lul - lul - lul - lul - lah.

lul - lul - lul - lul - lah ful-lul - lul - lul - lul - lul - lah.

lul - lul - lul - lul - lah ful-lul - lul - lul - lul - lul - lah.

lul - lul - lul' - lul - lah ful-lul - lul - lul - lul - lul - lah.

And to the bag - pipe's sound The nymphs tread out the
ah - (nd) too thuh bah-(g)pah - (eeps) sah-(oond) thuh nih-(mfs) treh(d) ah-(oot) thuh

And to the bag - pipe's sound The nymphs tread out the
ah - (nd) too thuh bah - (g) pah-(eeps) sah-(oond) thuh nih-(mfs) treh(d) ah-(oot) thuh

And to the bag - pipe's sound The nymphs tread out the
ah - (nd) too thuh bah-(g)pah - (eeps) sah-(oond) thuh nih-(mfs) treh(d) ah-(oot) thuh

And to the bag - pipe's sound The nymphs tread out the
ah - (nd) too thuh bah-(g)pah - (eeps) sah-(oond) thuh nih-(mfs) treh(d) ah-(oot) thuh

And to the bag - pipe's sound The nymphs tread out the
ah - (nd) too thuh bah-(g)pah - (eeps) sah-(oond) thuh nih-(mfs) treh(d) ah-(oot) thuh

35
ff
p
sweet de-light re - fus - ing? ful-lul - lul - lul - lul - lul -
swee - (t)dee - lah - (eet)ree - f(ee)oo - (z)ih - (ng)
sweet de-light re - fus - ing? ful-lul - lul - lul-lul - lul -
sweet de-light re - fus - ing? ful-lul - lul - lul - lul - lul -
pp
40
lul - lul - lah, ful-lul - lul-lul-lul - lul - lah
lah, ful-lul-lah, ful-lul - lul-lul-lul - lul - lah
lah, ful-lul - lul-lul-lul - lul - lah
Say, dain - ty nymphs, and
say - (ee)day-(een)tee nih-(mfs) ah - (n

Chapter XVII

PRESSURE ACCENT

Roundelay—Clément Jannequin (16th Century)

DYNAMIC accents, although used by all instruments, including the voice, have been described as typical of percussion instruments. But percussion instruments are unable to increase the volume of sound after a tone has been started. This ability to produce a swell by enlarging and reducing the volume on a sustained tone is one of the characteristics of string and wind instruments. It is particularly useful with the voice.

If a singer breathes correctly, and produces his tones easily, the volume of tone he produces will be flexible, responding instantly to every wave of artistic feeling. The tone of a good singer ebbs and flows without conscious effort on his part.

Aside from these automatic increases and relaxations of breath pressure, there are times when certain tones are "pressed into prominence" by the breath. This is a form of accent which is typical of vocal technique. It is more vocal in character than the dynamic accent. The pressure accent should be used abundantly by the vocalist.

The principal subject of this jolly piece has two tones that are treated with pressure accents. The soprano starts on the third beat of the first measure:

The tenor starts on the second beat with the same rhythm although the melodic curve is somewhat different at the end:

These pressure accents occur on the most important syllables of the text, "sing" and "round." The composer has pushed these tones into the foreground by making them the highest tones in the phrase and by making them of longer duration than the other tones in the melody. We carry the good work further by increasing the prominence of these tones by pressure accents.

As this melody appears 24 times, either completely or in an

abbreviated form, during the course of the composition, there are numerous opportunities to study the pressure accent effect in this two-measure melody.

But this type of pressure accent is found at other places in this composition. There is a delightful contrast in the soprano part between the dynamic accent in the third measure and the pressure accent on the same tone in the fourth measure. Alto, tenor and bass all have the same contrast in types of accent in measures 3 and 4. The bass in particular has splendid opportunity to illustrate the two different types of accents when he repeats his melodic figure in measures 3 and 4. The same contrast appears in measures 7-8, 29-30, 33-34, 55-56, 59-60.

The charming cross-accents in this piece make it a delightful predecessor for Chapters XVIII, XX, XXI and XXII. Bar lines lose their importance in music of this type. Accent is the thing. It may be agogic, dynamic, or occasioned by important words or breath pressure. In any case it is the rhythm of the melody that is given prominence, while the metrical 1, 2, 3, 4 of each measure retires into the background.

Measures 1-10 are filled with these playful cross-accents as first one voice and then another accents the important tones in its melodies. Sopranos must be light and flexible, altos rich and full, tenors bright and clear, while the basses are resonant and big. What opportunity for sonorous resonance and dignity as the bass sings measures 3-4, especially when he drops down to D at the beginning of measure 4! The bass has the same opportunity later in the piece when these measures are repeated several times.

The first of the nonsense syllables is always printed as "trul," indicating a quick return of the tongue to the base of the upper teeth. In some cases this may not be desirable. For example, the alto in measure 4 has a pressure accent in the form of a swell on this syllable. The desired effect is attained more easily if the tone is kept open as though spelled "truh" or "trah." At the same time the tenor is singing "lul." He may find it more practical to sing "luh" or "lah" at this point. In measure 3 the tenors and the basses may prefer to hold the dotted quarter-notes open and sustained by singing "truh" or "trah" instead of "trul." The singer must use discretion with these nonsense syllables so they will be sprightly without eliminating the possibility of occasional sustained tones.

There are numerous opportunities to test the intonation. At the beginning, F and C are the most important foundation tones for pitch. Bass, tenor and alto, all start on F and move to C for their second tone. They can imitate each other in pitch. The sopranos have C for their second tone but they start on G. In measures 3 and

4, the sopranos and tenors test their *D* and *C*. The whole phrase repeats, beginning in measure 5, with a cadence in measure 9-10, affording opportunity for alto and bass to tune *C* and then soprano, tenor and bass can tune *F*. The imitations between men's and women's voices in measures 22-23 are easily tuned. Measures 25-26 are dangerous. Soprano and tenor sing the same tones except for alternating them. Practice these two parts together. The alto and bass sing the same tone and, consequently, they can tune perfectly.

Treat the *r* sound playfully in the words, "merry," "roundelay," and "trul-lul." Let the tip of the tongue roll the *r* at the front of the mouth with a trill against the back of the upper teeth. This promotes relaxation of the tongue and the vocal organs.

Come to a dignified close in measure 10 without too much *rallentando* in the previous measure.

In measure 10, the trebles will leave their tone immediately at the end of two beats. The tenors and basses will hold their tone on a smooth unison through the entire measure until after the trebles have sung their quarter-note on the fourth beat. But the tenors and basses must slide into the background on this fourth beat, and although they close their tone together, it should not be quitted abruptly.

Soprano and alto parts should be sung simply, daintily, and distinctly. There is excellent opportunity to tune as the alto and soprano trade tones at the start of their duets. Tune the perfect fifth at the beginning of measure 12 and the unison in measure 13.

The men's voices imitate with all the accuracy possible. Then the treble voices repeat very definitely and positively, and somewhat louder.

A *ritardando* is indicated in measure 12. The same passage and *ritardando* appear in measures 15 and 17. In order to avoid monotony, begin the *ritardando* one beat later in each case. In the first instance it begins at the crest of the melodic curve. In measure 17 it begins on the fourth beat which is the second beat beyond the melodic crest. This last *ritardando* affects only two chords, and merely gives dignity to the first beat of measure 18.

Note the dynamic accent in measure 18 which consists of a sudden, abrupt attack on a soft chord. The measure then trips along over some rather *staccato* eighth-notes but measure 19 is very smooth and boasts a luscious swell.

Do not exaggerate the *rallentando* in measure 21. Observe the dynamic accents in measures 22-23. Measure 24 is slightly slower and much bigger than what has gone before, as it prepares the way for the jolly, lively nonsense syllables which are sung softly but quickly in measures 25-26.

The end of measure 26 and beginning of measure 27 must be

handled gracefully to bring the music back to exactly the original tempo at the middle of measure 27.

Sing the final two measures boldly and resolutely with a firm, resonant tone as an impressive ending for a charming piece.

Aside from its musical charm, this piece may be used as an exercise to develop certain features of vocal technique. One of the most difficult letters to sing is *r*. It has a tendency to be gutteral, smothered and unpleasant in tone quality, at the same time tightening the muscles of the throat, tongue, and jaw. To avoid this, the *r* must be sung at the front of the mouth with a light, free, flexible tongue, producing a light trill. This can be practiced on the words "mer-ry," "roundelay," and the nonsense syllable "trul." Attention to the trill on these *r* sounds will loosen the vocal mechanism, bring the tone forward in the mouth, and add distinction to the singing.

Some conductors may wish to exaggerate the *ng* sound in the word "sing." This is a legitimate effect if the *ng* is really given enough energy to make it spin. Other conductors will defer the *ng* until the very end of the tone in order to make the most effective swell on the syllable "sih."

The *ay* vowel as in "say" has been described as consisting of two consecutive sounds, *ay* and *ee*. The *ee* is most prominent when the voice is moving without interruption to another sound. For example, the word "maid" is spelled phonetically, may-eed. The *ee* is least prominent when there is no sound following the *ay*. In this song the words "roundelay," "day," "gay," "away," all precede a rest. In these cases the *ee* is not added to the *ay* in the phonetic spelling. This suggests the desirability of holding the vocal position without change but it may be necessary to introduce a slight *ee* at the end of these tones to give character to the words.

ROUNDELAY

Translated by E. H. Wilcox

CLÉMENT JANNEQUIN
(16th Century)
Edited by E. H. Wilcox

77384-11

Tempo I
rit.
lah, trul-lul-lul-lul-lul-lul - lah. I sing a mer-ry round - e-
ah - (ee)sih - (ng)uh meh-ree rah - (oond) ee-
lah, trul-lul-lul-lul-lul-lul - lah. I sing a round-e-
ah - (ee) sih - (ng)uh rah-(oond)ee-
lah, trul-lul-lul-lul-lul-lul - lah. I sing a mer-ry round - e-lay,
ah-(ee)sih - (ng)uh meh-ree rah - (oond) ee - lay
lah, trul-lul-lul-lul-lul-lul - lah. I sing a round - e - lay,
ah-(ee)sih - (ng)uh rah-(oond)ee - lay
30
mf
lay, trul - lul - lul - lah, trul- lul - lul - lah, I sing
lay ah - (ee)sih -
lay, trul - lul-lul-lul - lah, trul - lul-lah, trul - lul-lah,
lay
trul - lul-lul - lah, trul - lul - lul-lah, I sing a
ah - (ee)sih - (ng)uh
trul - lul-lul - lah, trul - lul-lul - lah, I sing a round - e-
ah-(ee)sih - (ng)uh rah-(oond)ee-

— a mer-ry round - e - lay, trul - lul - lul - lah, trul - lul - lul -
(ng)uh meh-ree rah - (oond)ee - lay
mf
I sing a round - e - lay, trul - lul-lul-lul lah, trul - lul-lah,
ah - (ee)sih - (ng)uh rah-(oond)ee - lay
mer-ry round - e - lay, trul - lul-lul - lah, trul-lul - lul - lah, -
meh-ree rah - (oond)ee - lay
lay, trul - lul-lul -
lay
Meno mosso
35
rall.
f
p dolce
rit.
lah, trul-lul-lah-lah - lah. She said she might some oth - er
shee seh-(d)shee mah - (eet)suh-(m)uh-thuh-(r)
trul - lul - lah-lah - lah. She said she might some oth - er
shee seh-(d)shee mah - (eet)suh-(m)uh-thuh-(r)
— trul-lul - lah - lah.
lah, trul - lah-lah - lah.
Meno mosso
rit.

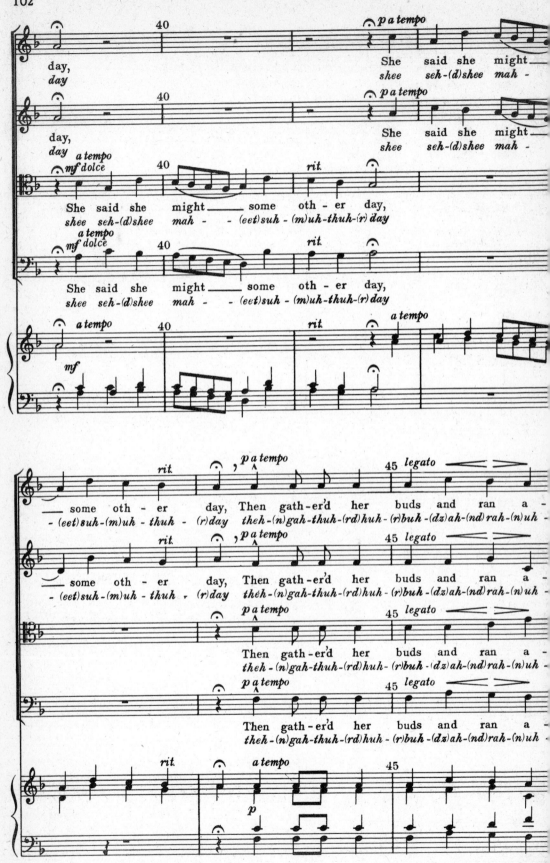

lah, I sing a merry round - e -
ah - (ee) sih - (ng) uh meh - ree rah - (oond) ee -

trul - lul - lah, I sing a round - e -
ah - (ee) sih - (ng) uh rah-(oond) ee -

I sing a mer-ry round - e - lay,
ah - (ee) sih - (ng) uh meh - ree rah - (oond) ee - lay

lah, I sing a round - e - lay,
ah-(ee) sih - (ng) uh rah-(oond) ee - lay

60

lay, trul - lul - lul - lah, trul - lul - lul - lah, trul-lul-lah-lah- lah.
lay

lay, trul - lul-lul-lul - lah, trul - lul-lah, trul - lul - lah-lah - lah.
lay

trul - lul-lul - lah, trul-lul - lul-lah, trul-lul - lah lah.

trul - lul-lul - lah, trul - lah-lah - lah.

CHAPTER XVIII

IMPORTANT WORD ACCENT

Lovely Lady—Orlando di Lasso (1532-1594)

IN GOOD choral singing, the important words always receive an accent. This accent may be of the dynamic, agogic, or pressure type.

The word or syllable "love" is stressed whenever it appears in this piece. In the first sentence, "Lovely lady like a lily," the syllable "love" receives a primary accent and "lil" has a secondary accent. The other words on eighth-notes are not stressed and "ly," coming at the end of the phrase, is sung with a falling inflection. When this sentence appears, it begins in the second soprano and alto with a primary accent on the second beat of the measure and a subordinate accent on the second beat of the following measure. First soprano, tenor and bass reply immediately, starting with a primary accent on the third beat of the measure and a subordinate accent on the third beat of the next measure. The second soprano and alto, not to be outdone, repeat the sentence, beginning this time on the fourth beat of measure 5, but even though this is the final beat of the measure, it receives the accent, the subordinate accent appearing on the fourth beat of the following measure. The three other voices repeat the sentence, beginning in measure 6 with the accent at last on the first beat of the measure.

The sentence "Love will only end in woe" is always accented on the words "love" and "woe," no matter on what part of the measure these words are found. In measure 9, the tenor begins the sentence on the fourth beat, consequently establishing an accent on the fourth beat in his part. The bass starts the same solo with an accent on the first beat of measure 10. The alto starts with a similar accent on the third beat, and the first soprano starts with an accent on the fourth beat of that measure.

The first and third lines of the words give opportunity to study the liquid vowel sounds. Especially the first line, with six *l* sounds, is an effectual exercise for these sounds. The last line is almost equally full of liquid vowels.

In the second line, do not fear to use the tongue, lips and cheeks. They should always be active and responsive. "Will not woo" gives the lips good exercise.

Good choral music for small groups maintains an individuality in each voice part. The spirit in a composition of this type is apparent when each part is sung with independence and character. If the singers will follow the parts, bringing out the accents with independence and vigor, the total result in the chorus will be the cross relation of accents, which gives great vitality and life to the rendition. This independence of parts is one of the distinguishing characteristics of the type of piece included in this chapter in contrast to the *Adoramus Te* of Chapter XIII.

Even in the "ful-lul-lul," a certain syllable must be given prominence. In this case it is the third syllable which invariably appears as the highest tone in the melodic curve. Make a short but positive swell with this tone accented as the climax of the swell, no matter on what beat of the measure it is found.

There are several other short swells of decided importance. The alto has one of these in measure 9. There is another and shorter one for the alto in measure 7. Measure 8 has a difficult place for the alto with the swell on a syncopation.

The humorous words indicate the whole piece is intended to be jolly and witty. The rapid imitation of voices in measures 1 and 2 suggests that the voices are expected to chase one another clear across the page. Do this chasing with zest in a jovial whole-hearted manner and the piece will disclose many charms.

The whole composition must be sung in a sprightly manner. Enunciate the consonants crisply to give a chattering, vivacious and sparkling effect. Keep it light and springing with an alert and bounding tongue. Speed, *staccato* attack, and lightness of style are essential.

Note that volume is not necessary for sprightliness. In fact, loud singing has a tendency to be heavy and inflexible, quite the opposite of what we want. Use a small amount of breath and strive for neatness, precision, accuracy, and charm.

The repetitions should be taken one degree softer than indicated for the first time through.

LOVELY LADY

English version by E. H. Wilcox

ORLANDO DI LASSO (1532-1594)
Edited by J. S. and E. H. W.

77384- 117

sf
love - ly la - dy like a lil - y, As for me,
luh - (v)lee lay - dee lah - (eek)uh lihl - ee ah - (z)faw - (r)mee
p
- ly la - dy like a lil - y, As for me,
- (v)lee lay - dee lah(eek)uh lihl - ee ah - (z)faw - (r)mee
- ly la - dy like a lil - y, As for me, I
- (v)lee lay - dee lah(eek)uh lihl - ee ah - (z)faw(r)mee ah - (ee)
sf
love - ly la - dy like a lil - y,
luh - (v)lee lay - dee lah - (eek)uh lihl - ee
sf
p
love - ly la - dy like a lil - y, As for me,
luh - (v)lee lay - dee lah - (eek)uh lihl - ee ah - (z)faw - (r)mee
I will not woo her, I will not woo her.
ah - (ee)wih - (l)naw - (t)woo huh - (r)ah - (ee)wih - (l)naw - (t)woo huh - (r)
I will not woo her, I will not woo her.
ah - (ee)wih - (l)naw - (t)woo huh - (r)ah - (ee)wih - (l)naw - (t)woo huh - (r)
will not woo her, I will not woo her.
wih - (l)naw - (t)woo huh - (r)ah - (ee)wih - (l)naw - (t)woo huh - (r)
mf sf
Love
Luh -
I will not woo her, I will not woo her.
ah - (ee)wih - (l)naw - (t)woo huh - (r)ah - (ee)wih - (l)naw - (t)woo huh - (r)
mf

mf sf
lul - lul - lul - lul - lul - lul - lul - lul - lah, Love - ly
luh - (v) lee
Love - ly la - dy
luh - (v) lee lay - dee
lul - lul - lul - lul - lah, Love - ly la - dy
luh - (v) lee lay - dee
ful - lul - lul - lah, Love - ly
luh - (v) lee
- lul - lul - lah, Love - ly
luh - (v) lee
mf
20
sf
la - dy like a lil - y, love - ly la - dy like a
lay - dee lah-(eek)uh lihl - ee luh - (v) lee lay - dee lah-(eek)uh
like a lil - y, love - ly la - dy like a lil -
lah-(eek)uh lihl - ee luh - (v) lee lay - dee lah-(eek)uh lihl -
like a lil - y, love - ly la - dy like a lil -
lah-(eek)uh lihl - ee luh - (v) lee lay - dee lah-(eek)uh lihl -
la - dy like a lil - y, love - ly la - dy like a
lay - dee lah-(eek)uh lihl - ee luh - (v) lee lay - dee lah-(eek)uh
la - dy like a lil - y, love - ly la - dy like a
lay - dee lah-(eek)uh lihl - ee luh - (v) lee lay - dee lah-(eek)uh

lil - y, As for me, I will not woo her, I
lihl - ee ah-(z) faw-(r)mee ah-(ee)wih-(l)naw(t)woo huh-(r)ah-(ee)
y, As for me, I will not woo her, I
ee ah-(z)faw-(r)mee ah-(ee)wih-(l)naw(t)woo huh-(r)ah-(ee)
y, As for me, I will not woo her,
ee ah-(z)faw(r)mee ah-(ee)wih - (l)naw-(t)woo huh -
lil - y,
lihl - ee
lil - y, As for me, I will not woo her, I
lihl - ee ah-(z)faw-(r)mee ah-(ee)wih-(l)naw(t)woo huh-(r)ah-(ee)
will not woo her. Love
wih-(l)naw-(t)woo huh - (r) luh -
will not woo her.
wih-(l)naw-(t)woo huh - (r)
I will not woo her. Love will
- (r) ah-(ee)wih(l)naw(t)woo huh - (r) luh - (v) wih-(l)
Love will on - ly end in woe,
luh - (v) wih-(l) oh-(n)lee eh-(nd) ih-(n)woh
will not woo her. Love will on - ly end in
wih-(l)naw-(t)woo huh - (r) luh - (v)wih-(l)oh - (n)lee eh-(nd) ih-(n)
25

30
mp
end in woe, ful - lul - lah, ful - lul - lul - lul -
eh - (nd) ih - n) woh
end in woe, ful - lul - lah,
end in woe,
end in woe, ful - lul - lul - lul - lul - lul - lah,
end in woe, ful - lul - lul - lul - lul - lul -
lul-lul - lah, ful-lul - lul-lul-lul-lul - lul-lul-lul-lul - lah.
ful-lul-lul-lul-lul-lul-lah, ful - lah - lah.
ful-lul-lul-lul-lul-lul - lul - lul - lul - lul - lah.
fah - lul - lul - lah.
lah - lah - lul - lul - lah.

Chapter XIX

THE SHAPE OF LONG PHRASES

Since First I Saw your Face—Thomas Ford (1580-1648)

ONE of the secrets of good choral singing is the ability to give shape to a long phrase or period. This number begins with a four-measure phrase which consists of a swell with its climax at the beginning of the third measure. A breath mark is indicated after the first beat of the second measure, but experienced singers will do the four measures in one breath, in order to round the phrase out as one complete swell without any breaks.

By the same token, the second group of four measures will be treated as one unit and sung on one breath, if convenient, even though a possible breathing place is indicated in measure 6 for those who find it desirable to breathe at frequent intervals.

Measures 9-12 constitute another four measure unit. It is much easier to sing this without interruption because the voices breathe at different times. The bass is always sustaining boldly while the others are breathing. This is a serviceable device which can be used often.

In measures 13-17 the five voices never breathe simultaneously, and consequently, the music can flow without a complete interruption. If desired, all voices may breathe after the final word "no." This will come at a different place in the men's and women's parts.

At times it is wise to guard against too much of a break between units. In measure 8, the bass sustains while the other three parts complete the word "you," take breath and begin the word "What." The bass can breathe while the other voices are singing "I."

The second verse includes a breath mark after "glorious are." In conformity with the suggestions for the first verse, it is better to omit this breath in order to make a continuously flowing four-measure unit, providing the singers have sufficient breath to sing this much without strain. If the breath is taken after "glorious are," it is effective to let the upper voices breathe while the bass sustains with a little extra pressure to cover the gap made by the upper voices. In such a case, the bass can breathe after "sun" if necessary to give him enough breath.

There is splendid opportunity to test the *n* resonance in the word "no." Give great vitality and concentration to this *n* sound.

The letter *r* causes difficulty in some words. In "heart" and "first," reduce the *r* sound to the vanishing point. This sound should be treated very lightly in such words as "never," "bolder," and "beholder."

116

"Glorious" is written in three syllables. The eighth-notes in the soprano parts can be produced more smoothly if the vowels of the ast two syllables are treated as a diphthong, moving quickly over *ree* and singing the two eighth-notes on *uh*. In that case the other voices will have a quarter-note for the second beat devoted entirely to the syllable *uhs*.

The opening chord has only two tones sounding. The women's voices are at a unison, doubling the bass an octave higher. The tenor has the other tone which is an open fifth above the bass. This must be sung very accurately in tune, with good resonance but not too loud, to give the desired effect.

The suspension in the tenor part in measure 4 must be sung accurately in tune in order to blend perfectly with the melody when the unison is reached on the third beat. The alto becomes supplementary to the melody from the third beat of measure 2 through measure 4. They must avoid undue prominence, but the tone must melt in with the melody without any abrupt intrusion, merely enriching and warming it. The second soprano must be extremely light and flute-like in measure 4. All of these suggestions apply as well to the second phrase of four measures and to the second verse.

Sopranos and tenors in measure 9 will be very careful to sing the *A♮* accurately in tune and sufficiently high in pitch to give a major effect to the chord.

The women's voices will be very resonant and prominent in measure 11. At this point the alto will use heavy chest tones as the composer originally intended these tones to be sung prominently by a high tenor voice.

There is a lovely *decrescendo* which must extend gradually from measure 13 to the end of the verse.

The second verse is sung much the same as the first, except for a slight dynamic change near the end.

This tenderly beautiful text owes much of its charm to the old expressions such as "honor and renown you." The entire poem breathes the spirit of chivalric antiquity.

SINCE FIRST I SAW YOUR FACE

Edited by E. H. Wilcox

THOMAS FORD (1580-1648)

77384-117

mf
mp
dain'd, I wish my heart had nev-er known you. What,
day-(nd)ah-(ee)wih-(sh)mah-(ee)hah-(rt)hah-(d)neh-(v)uh-(r)noh-(n)yoo whaw-(t)
dain'd, I wish my heart had nev-er known you. What,
day-(nd)ah-(ee)wih-(sh)mah-(ee)hah-(rt)hah-(d)neh-(v)uh-(r)noh-(n)yoo whaw-(t)
dain'd, I wish my heart had nev-er known you. What,
day-(nd)ah-(ee)wih-(sh)mah-(ee)hah-(rt)hah-(d)neh-(v)uh-(r)noh-(n)yoo whaw-(t)
dain'd, I wish my heart had nev-er known you. What,
day-(nd)ah-(ee)wih-(sh)mah-(ee)hah-(rt)hah-(d)neh-(v)uh-(r)noh-(n)yoo whaw-(t)
dain'd, I wish my heart had nev-er known you.
day-(nd)ah-(ee)wih-(sh)mah-(ee)hah-(rt)hah-(d)neh-(v)uh-(r)noh-(n)yoo
10
f
I that loved, and you that liked, shall we be-gin to wran-gle?
ah-(ee)thah(t)luh(vd)ah-(nd)yoo thah(t)lah(eekt)shah-(l)wee bee-gih-(n)too rah-(n)guh-(l)
I that loved, and you that liked, shall we be-gin to wran-gle?
ah-(ee)thah(t)luh(vd)ah-(nd)yoo thah(t)lah(eekt)shah-(l)wee bee-gih-(n)too rah-(n)guh-(l)
I that loved, and you that liked, shall we be-gin to wran-gle?
ah-(ee)thah(t)luh-(vd)ah(nd)yoo thah-(t)lah(eekt)shah-(l)wee bee-gih-(n)too rah-(n)guh-(l)
I that loved, and you that liked, shall we be-gin to wran-gle?
ah-(ee)thah(t)luh(vd)ah-(nd)yoo thah-(t)lah(eekt)shah-(l)wee bee-gih(n)too rah-(n)guh-(l)
What, I that loved, and you that liked, shall we wran-gle?
whaw-(t)ah-(ee)thah-(t)luh(vd)ah(nd)yoo thah(t)lah(eekt)shah-(l)wee rah-(n)guh-(l)

No, no, no! My heart is fast And can - not
noh noh noh mah-(ee)hah - (rt)ih - (s)fah - (st)ah - (nd)kah - (n)naw -
No, no, no, no, no! My heart is fast And can - not
noh noh noh noh noh mah - (ee)hah - (rt)ih - (s)fah - (st)ah - (nd)kah - (n)naw -
No, no, no! My heart is fast And can - not dis -
noh noh noh mah - (ee)hah - (rt)ih - (s)fah - (st)ah - (nd)kah - (n)naw - (t)dih -
dis - en - tan - gle. No, no,
dih - (s)eh - (n)tah - (n)guh - (l) noh noh
dis- en- tan - gle. No, no, no, no,
dih- (s)eh- (n)tah - (n)guh - (l) noh noh noh noh
en - tan - gle. No, no, no! My
(s)eh - (n)tah - (n)guh - (l) noh noh noh mah - (ee)

ject - eth no be - hold - er; And your sweet beau - ty
jeh - (k)teh-(th)noh bee - hoh - (ld)uh - (r)ah - (nd)yoo - (r)swee - (t)b(ee)oo - tee
ject - eth no be - hold - er; And your sweet beau - ty
jeh - (k)teh-(th)noh bee - hoh - (ld)uh - (r)ah - (nd)yoo - (r)swee - (t)b(ee)oo - tee
ject - eth no be - hold - er; And your sweet beau - ty
jeh - (k)teh-(th)noh bee - hoh - (ld)uh - (r)ah - (nd)yoo - (r)swee - (t)b(ee)oo - tee
ject - eth no be - hold - er; And your sweet beau - ty
jeh - (k)teh - (th)noh bee - hoh - (ld)uh - (r)ah - (nd)yoo - (r)swee - (t)b(ee)oo - tee
ject - eth no be - hold - er; And your sweet beau - ty
jeh - (k)teh-(th)noh bee - hoh - (ld)uh - (r)ah - (nd)yoo - (r)swee - (t)b(ee)oo - tee
30
past com - pare Made my poor eyes the bold - er. Where
pah-(st)kuh-(m)pay-(eer)may - (eed)mah - (ee)poo - (r)ah - (eez)thuh boh - (ld)uh - (r)wheh - (r
past com - pare Made my poor eyes the bold - er. Where
pah-(st)kuh-(m)pay-(eer)may - (eed)mah - (ee)poo - (r)ah - (eez)thuh boh - (ld)uh - (r)wheh - (r
past com - pare Made my poor eyes the bold - er. Where
pah-(st)kuh-(m)pay-(eer)may - (eed)mah - (ee)poo - (r)ah - (eez)thuh boh - (ld)uh - (r)wheh - (r
past com - pare. Made my poor eyes the bold - er. Where
pah-(st)kuh-(m)pay-(eer)may - (eed)mah-(ee)poo - (r)ah - (eez)thuh boh - (ld)uh - (r)wheh - (r
past com - pare. Made my poor eyes the bold - er.
pah-(st)kuh-(m)pay-(eer)may - (eed)mah - (ee)poo - (r)ah - (eez)thuh boh - (ld)uh - (r)

beau - ty moves, and wit de - lights, And signs of kind - ness
b(ee)oo - tee moo-(vz)ah - (nd)wih - (t)dee-lah-(eets)ah - (nd)sah - (eenz)aw-(v)kah-(eend)neh - (s)

beau - ty moves, and wit de - lights, And signs of kind - ness
b(ee)oo - tee moo-(vz)ah - (nd)wih - (t)dee-lah-(eets) ah - (nd)sah - (eenz)aw-(v)kah-(eend) neh - (s)

beau - ty moves, and wit de - lights, And signs of kind - ness
b(ee)oo - tee moo - (vz) ah (nd)wih-(t)dee - lah-(eets)ah - (nd)sah-(eenz)aw - (v)kah-(eend)neh - (s)

beau - ty moves, and wit de - lights, And signs of kind - ness
b(ee)oo - tee moo-(vz)ah-(nd)wih-(t)dee - lah-(eets)ah - (nd)sah-(eenz)aw - (v)kah-(eend)neh - (s)

Where beau - ty moves, and wit de - lights, And
wheh-(r)b(ee)oo - tee moo-(vz)ah-(nd)wih - (t)dee - lah-(eets)ah - - (nd)

bind me, There, O there! Wher-e'er I go, I leave my
bah-(eend)mee theh- (r)oh theh- (r)wheh(r)eh - (r)ah-(ee)goh ah-(ee)lee-(v)mah(ee)

bind me, There, O there! Wher-e'er I go, I leave my
bah-(eend)mee theh- (r)oh theh- (r)wheh(r)eh - (r)ah-(ee)goh ah-(ee)lee-(v)mah(ee)

bind me, There, O there, O there! Wher-e'er I go, I leave my
bah-(eend)mee theh-(r)oh theh-(r)oh theh-(r)wheh-(r)eh-(r)ah-(ee)goh ah-(ee)lee-(v)mah(ee)

bind me, There, O there! Wher-e'er I go, I leave my heart
bah-(eend)mee theh-(r) oh theh-(r)wheh-(r)eh - (r)ah-(ee)goh ah-(ee)lee-(v)mah-(ee)hah -

bind me, There, O there! Wher - e'er I go, I leave my heart
bah-(eend)mee theh- (r) oh theh-(r)wheh-(r)eh - (r)ah-(ee)goh ah-(ee)lee-(v)mah-(ee)hah -

40
mp
heart be - hind me. There, O there! wher - e'er I
hah - (rt)bee - hah - (eend) mee theh - (r)oh theh - (r)wheh-(r)eh - (r)ah-(e
heart be - hind me. There, O there! wher - e'er I
hah - (rt)bee - hah - (eend) mee theh - (r)oh theh - (r)wheh-(r)eh - (r)ah-(e
heart be - hind me. There, O there! O there! wher - e'er I
hah - (rt)bee - hah-(eend) mee theh-(r)oh theh-(r)oh theh-(r)wheh-(r)eh - (r)ah-(e
be - hind me. There, O there! wher - e'er I go, I
- (rt)bee-hah - (eend) mee theh - (r)oh theh-(r)wheh - (r)eh - (r)ah-(ee)goh ah - (ee
be - hind me. There, O there! wher - e'er I go, I
- (rt)bee-hah - (eend) mee theh - (r)oh theh-(r)wheh - (r)eh - (r)ah-(ee)goh ah - (ee
pp
go, I leave my heart be - hind me.
goh ah - (ee)lee - (v)mah - (ee)hah - (rt)bee - hah - (eend) mee
go, I leave my heart be - hind me.
goh ah - (ee)lee - (v)mah - (ee)hah - (rt)bee - hah - (eend) mee
go, I leave my heart be - hind me.
goh ah - (ee)lee - (v)mah - hah - (rt)bee - hah-(eend) mee
leave my heart be - hind me.
lee - (v)mah - (ee)hah - - (rt)bee - hah - (eend) mee
leave my heart be - hind me.
lee - (v)mah - (ee)hah - - (rt)bee - hah - (eend) mee

CHAPTER XX

THE SHAPE OF SHORT PHRASES

Fields of Green and Gold— Giovanni P. da Palestrina (1514?-1594)

Tʜɪs madrigal consists of rather short phrases, five of which will be chosen to illustrate the form of short phrases. Although the first melody covers four and a half measures, this is only nine beats as opposed to the sixteen beats of the first phrase in the preceding chapter. Our first phrase is as follows:

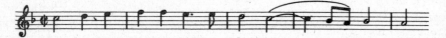

Although it may be varied in the time-value of some of its notes, the melody is always one curve, a rising inflection to a climax and then a falling inflection which can be depicted graphically as:

A swell is invariably found on this phrase, so it should be pictured

thus: The swell is as much a part of the

music as the notes themselves. There are no decided accents, merely a graceful swell. The phrase will have no character if it is not properly shaped every time it is heard, even in an abridged form. This phrase is smooth, flowing, sustained and graceful. It always progresses scalewise as it has no skips.

Our second example is quite the reverse, for it is abrupt, accented, terse and vigorous. It consists entirely of skips, not once moving scale-wise from a tone to its neighboring scale degree.

The character of this phrase lies in its accents and its skips, gradually working upward chord-wise to its strongly accented top tone. This phrase must be given definite character to produce sufficient contrast to the first phrase.

Our next phrase is a combination of scale-wise and chord-wise movement.

The *staccato* notes give this phrase a decidedly different quality from those preceding. Its shape is determined by the slightly accented first tone, the tripping *staccato* quarter-notes, and the final accent with immediate *diminuendo*. This phrase is lithe with no bulges and no sharp corners.

Beginning with the fourth beat of measure 21, we have a joyful phrase, consisting of one upward leap and a descending scale.

This is almost martial in character. It begins with a strongly accented fourth beat, followed by a series of energetic tones, forming a slight swell as the melody skips upward. Here we have a swell combined with vigorous treatment.

Starting at measure 31, there is a phrase which contrasts sharply with any listed above. It glides and slides along its smooth and sinuous way as though it were the wind. There is only a small pitch range as this phrase is like a slightly curved horizontal line.

There must be some flexibility or "give-and-take" in the eighth-note runs, increasing the breath pressure slightly on the ascending scales and decreasing the pressure on the descending scales. This will give the sinuous character required by this phrase.

So all of these phrases have an individual shape and style which give them character. The distinctness with which they are outlined by the singers has much to do with the effectiveness of the chorus.

Recognition of these phrase shapes will give an insight into the expression for this piece. The first phrase opens with the soprano in the first measure. Although this voice starts *mf* it immediately begins the characteristic swell. This makes it necessary for the alto to start *f* in the second measure. Avoid a scratchy tone.

The tenors begin *mf* in the fourth measure, but the basses are compelled to sing *f* in measure 5. Listen intently to the *ee* sound in the words "knee-deep," "fields," and "green." These sounds give an unusual opportunity for a concentrated, brilliant tone if it is kept free, easy, and open without any strain or stridency.

In measure 8, the bass sustains firmly, but the tenor is soft and the other two voices are diminishing to let the next phrase enter prominently. The tenor starts this vigorous phrase on the beginning of measure 9 to be imitated by the bass one measure later. But in the meantime, the treble voices have become impatient, so the soprano enters on the last quarter of measure 9 and the alto imitates her on the last quarter of measure 10.

It is interesting to note the upward skip of an octave in the bass on the second and third quarters of measure 11, followed by the same octave skip in the alto one octave higher from the fourth quarter of measure 11 to the first quarter of measure 12.

The quarter-notes in measure 16 and their imitation in measure 17 are marked *staccato*. This is correct musically but it is very difficult vocally because the (*ee*), (*n*) and (*een*) tend to bind the syllables together.

The alto will treat measure 21 very delicately when it crosses the soprano part to reach *C*. This tone must not be too loud. It should be the softest tone in the chord.

The *tenuto* in measure 28 is important. Stress the *Eb* in alto and bass, tuning this octave carefully and holding the other tones of the chord well in tune. Let the chord resound its full time-value as though it were hard to move on. In fact, a suspicion of a *ritard.* beginning on the third quarter of measure 27 is quite correct. But the tempo must be resumed briskly on the third quarter of measure 28.

From the middle of measure 28 to the beginning of measure 31 the parts move in pairs: the soprano and tenor, and the alto and bass. The first pair makes its introductory leap to an accent and then diminishes while the other pair swells.

The running passages on the word "follow" need to be very clean. The voices touch only the notes printed, without sliding from one tone to the other.

Measure 37 is full of fun, the tenor starting his scale on the first quarter, the alto following on the second quarter and the soprano entering on the third quarter. Each of these entrances must be positive, clean, and distinct to bring out the idea of imitation.

At measure 40, the chord swells with a slight push of breath, almost as though the whole chorus were sighing. This same effect appears always on the word "soothing."

Toward the close the most difficult word is "desire." Sustain the *ah* with no suspicion of *eer* until the very end of the tone. The soprano could ruin the ending by letting the *eer* creep into the next to the last measure too soon.

The bass is rather prominent in the last five measures and the alto sings her *Eb tenuto* in the next to the last measure.

The last twenty measures are smooth and quiet, leading to a peaceful and poetic close.

Although the metronome speed is given as ninety half-notes to the minute, some conductors prefer the more leisurely tempo of about sixty half-notes to the minute.

FIELDS OF GREEN AND GOLD

English version by E. H. Wilcox

GIOVANNI P. da PALESTRINA
Edited by E. H. W.

77384-117

THE SHAPE OF COMPLETE PIECES

I Only Weep—Mathieu Gascongne (Early 16th Century)

THERE are five chief melodies in this piece. I shall call each melody a "subject" because it is presented many times in a constantly changing musical setting so that the subject is "developed" to have more significance for the hearer at the end of the piece than it had when first sung.

The principal subject is comparatively long, covering four measures. Essentially it consists of *mi-re-do* in the following form:

But in order to accommodate words and to add the beauty of simple adornment, this subject is embellished as follows:

This subject appears three times in the soprano in measure 9-12, 12-15, 20-23 and once in the tenor in measures 16-19. By virtue of this character and use, this subject might be called the "plain song" or "cantus" to which other melodies as "counterpoints" or "countersubjects" are added.

It must be sung in an even, sustained, *legato* style in conformity with the simple *mi-re-do* from which it is derived.

The other subjects are short. One is four tones, the first three in an ascending scale and the fourth dropping back to the same pitch as the first. The first tone is a quarter-note and the others are half-notes.

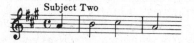

The soprano has this subject in measures 1-3, 3-5, 23-25 and 25-27. The alto sings it in measures 1-2 and, in a slightly altered form, in measures 23-25 and 25-27.

At first this subject is set to slow, sad words, "I only weep," but when it appears later with the words "My bright and gay companion," the half-notes are broken into quarter-notes, giving the more hopeful rhythm:

In this form the soprano sings the subject in measures 31-33, 33-35, 38-39, 40-42, 46-47 and 48-50. The alto uses the same subject greatly quickened in measures 3-4.

Another subject, consisting of four tones, drops down two degrees between the first and second tones and then ascends scalewise to the point of origin. The first tone is a quarter-note, and the second a dotted quarter-note, the third an eighth-note, and the fourth may be a quarter-note or a tone of longer duration. This subject does not stop abruptly but continues in various melodic lines. Its simplest form is as follows:

The alto sings this subject in measures 9-10. It is in the bass in measures 12-13, 16-17, 20-21, and slightly varied in measures 31-32 and 33-34.

A fourth subject consists of four tones, beginning with an upward skip of four degrees, followed by a downward scale passage of three tones. Occasionally the upward skip is five degrees. The final tone has various time-values. The three first tones may be even or varied as shown:

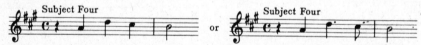

It is found in the tenor of measures 1-2, 3-4, and the bass of measures 2-3, 4-5, 5-6, 38-39, 39-40, 40-41, 41-42, 46-47, 47-48, 48-49, and 49-50. The fifth subject is merely four tones in the following form:

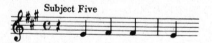

The final tone may be of any duration necessary to connect with the melodic line which continues from it. The tenor sings the subject in measures 12-13, 20-21, and the alto uses it in measures 15-16 and 19-20. This subject is extended into the following shapes:

In these forms it is found in the tenor of measures 30-32, 32-34, 38-40, 41-42, 46-48, 49-50; and the alto in measures 30-32, 32-34.

Derivatives of these subjects appear in other measures in addition to those listed.   Even this short analysis demonstrates how a composer utilizes a small amount of carefully selected, beautiful material to build a large composition.

In the subsequent discussion the five subjects will be designated by number in the order in which they were introduced above.

Musical compositions, like pictures, are usually set in a frame, consisting of an introduction and a conclusion.   Our introduction is eight measures and the conclusion is three measures.   As measures 46-53 are merely repetitions of the previous eight measures, they do not affect the structure of our piece.   Therefore the skeleton of the structure is as follows:

Introduction	Main Body	Conclusion
1-8	9-45	54-56

But the "main body" of 37 measures consists of two 15-measure sections which develop the themes.   These two sections are separated by 7 measures of interlude.   This gives us a structure as follows:—

Introduction	Main Body			Conclusion
	First Section	Interlude	Second Section	
1-8	9-23	24-30	31-45	54-56

The introduction establishes the key, measure, tempo and style. It also introduces two of the subjects.   Subject Two is heard four times and subject Four is heard five times.   Each voice has the responsibility of at least two statements of a subject.

The first section of the main body begins at measure 9 with Subject One in the soprano and Subject Three simultaneously in the alto. This beginning is very simple with only two voices singing.

At measure 12, Subject One is repeated in the soprano, this time in conjunction with Subject Three in the bass and Subject Five in the tenor, all four voices singing.

The tenor announces Subject One in measure 16, while the alto completes Subject Five and the bass sings Subject Three.   This is for three voices as a contrast.

But all four voices join in measure 20, the soprano singing Subject One, the alto completing Subject Five, the tenor starting Subject Five, and the bass singing Subject Three.

The interlude in measures 24-30 has the same soprano as the introduction but the other voices are different.   They do not busy themselves with the subjects as the interlude is a point of rest and relaxation.

Prominence should be given to the alto part in the interlude. It has a rising minor third which fits the character of the passage.

The second section, beginning with the last quarter-note in measure 30, presents the subjects in a new version of increased vigor. Subjects Two, Three and Five are treated simultaneously. Beginning at measure 38, Subjects Two, Four and Five are treated simultaneously.

The conclusion is a stately moving cadence which is merely a repetition of the three preceding measures.

The general structure of the entire piece can be indicated in letters as follows:

Introduction	Main Body		
	First Development Section	Interlude	Second Development Section
A	B	A′	B′

A more complete structural analysis, recognizing the cadences would be as follows:

Introduction		First Development Section			
Subjects	Cadence	Subjects	Subjects	Subjects	Subjects
Measures 1-5	6-8	9-12	12-15	15-19	19-23

Interlude			Second Development Section			
Subject	Subject	Cadence	Subjects	Cadence	Subjects	Cadence
23-25	25-27	27-30	30-35	35-37	37-42	42-45

Repetition		Conclusion
Subjects	Cadence	Cadence
45-50	50-53	53-56

Observe the simplicity with which the melodic material is presented for first hearing, with the gradual increase in complexity as the melodies are piled one on top of the other to be heard simultaneously. This gradually increasing intensity leads to a conclusion in that marvelously strong cadence in measures 43-45, 51-53, 54-56, with the firm descending scales in soprano and bass and the moving inner voices.

Note how the subjects are presented in various combinations for the purpose of contrast. Recognize the symmetry and balance in the development of the subjects as the piece grows from beginning to end.

An understanding and appreciation of the workmanship and art of a composer in building a composition in which every detail is a perfect and essential part of the whole, is one of the great sources of joy to the music student.

Analyze the structure of every piece you sing. It is immaterial what terms you use to describe the forms or their elements. The important point is to notice the structural details of each piece. Every piece will be recognized as different from every other piece in this regard, yet running through them all, the observer will discover certain basic principles of structure and design.

In the first measures the bass and tenor reply to each other, using Subject Four. This imitation between these two voices must be very apparent. At the same time, the soprano and alto are imitating each other, using Subject Two.

The tenor is important in the first measure. He must give a graceful swell to Subject Four which will be imitated by the bass. Listen intently to the vowels and consonants. In the pronoun "I," stress the *ah* for practically the entire value of the note. *Ee* is so short it is almost eliminated, but what there is left of it remains on the same pitch as *ah*. The next syllable begins with a vowel so there must be a very smooth and quick shift to the pitch of *oh*. The *n* remains on the pitch of *oh*, but the *l* has the pitch of the following *ee*. That is, the pitch changes between *n* and *l*. As these are both liquid consonants, it is necessary to change pitch and consonants simultaneously and quickly. The *w* of "weep" is on the pitch of the following *ee*. The *p* should be saved until the end of the duration of the note. Accurate attention to details in the first few measures will give the piece a proper start.

After each voice has sung one of the subjects twice, the music becomes very sustained in all voices from measure 5 to 9.

Guard against difficulties in the word "joys." Sustain the *aw*. Do not permit the *eez* to intrude. Hold the vowel sound *aw* without change until the very end of the tone.

The altos have an awkward part in measure 13 on the word "of" which comes on the first of the measure. Give it a broad *aw* sound

Every one will need to watch the word "turned" with its unpleasant *r* trying to intrude on the *uh*.

In measure 19, the bass must surely sustain a full measure although the tenors quit the same tone after the second beat.

The altos should swell prominently in measures 23-25 and 25-27. These chords are like great sighs on the words "I only weep," followed by a sustained passage in measures 28-30.

A curious section begins in measure 38. The soprano and alto seem to take a pleasant delight in the happy memory of the charming companion whom they describe as "bright and gay." But this cheerful, tripping idea in the treble stands in contrast to the sweetly solemn declaration of the bass, "I only weep," and the confession of the tenor (Is he sincere?), "My sad heart cries for thee."

The piece closes with a sustained expression of the wish that the companion could return.

I ONLY WEEP
(Je ne saurais chanter ni rire)

English version by E. H. Wilcox

MATHIEU GASCONGNE
Early 16th Century
Edited by E. H. W.

77384-1

only weep, My sad heart cries for thee,
oh - (n)lee wee - (p) mah-(ee)sah - (d)hah - (rt)krah-(eez)faw-(r)thee

_ on - ly weep, My sad heart cries_ for thee, My
- (ee) oh-(n)lee wee - (p) mah-(ee)sah - (d)hah-(rt)krah-(eez)faw - (r)thee mah-(ee)

on - ly weep, My sad heart cries_ for thee, My
oh - (n)lee wee - (p) mah-(ee)sah - (d)hah-(rt)krah-(eez)faw - (r)thee mah-(ee)

on - ly weep, My sad heart cries_ for thee, _
oh - (n)lee wee-(p)mah-(ee)sah - (d)hah-(rt)krah-(eez)faw - (r)thee

My bright and gay com - pan - ion, My
mah - (ee)brah-(eet)ah-(nd)gay-(ee)kaw-(m)pah-(n)yuh - (n) mah-(ee)

bright and gay com - pan - ion, My bright and gay com-
brah-(eet)ah - (nd)gay - (ee)kaw-(m)pah - (n)yuh-(n)mah-(ee)brah-(eet)ah - (nd)gay - (ee)kaw(m)

bright and gay com - pan - ion, My bright and gay com-
brah - (eet)ah(nd)gay-(ee)kaw - (m)pah - (n)yuh-(n)mah-(ee)brah - (eet)ah(nd)gay-(ee)kaw-(m)

My bright and gay com - pan - ion, My bright and
mah-(ee)brah-(eet)ah - (nd)gay-(ee)kaw(m)pah-(n)yuh - (n) mah-(ee)brah-(eet)ah-(nd)

* In measures 30-34 the original Alto and Tenor parts have been interchanged for practicability in this edition.

Chapter XXII

RHYTHMIC VARIETY

Fair Phyllis—John Farmer (fl. 1591-1601)

This charming madrigal by John Farmer shows how various rhythms may be used for a single section of the text. Four examples are chosen from this piece. The numbers refer to the measures and the letters refer to the voice parts as follows: S—Soprano, A—Alto, T—Tenor, B—Bass. The vertical dotted lines indicate the position of the bar lines.

The following section of the text is given first because it has the same rhythm for all voices. The only variation is in the position of the bar line.

whith-er she was gone

♪ ♪ ♪ ♪ | ♩   S 15-16 A 15-16

| ♪ ♪ ♪ ♪ ♩   T 17 B 17

The next is a unit which is only slightly changed in its four repetitions.

The Shep-herds knew not

♩ | ♩. ♪ ♩ ♪   S 13-14

♩ ♩. ♪ | ♩ ♪   T 15-16

♩ ♩. ♪ | ♩ ♩   A 14-15

♩ | ♩. ♪ ♩ ♩   B 15-16

The next phrase appears in six different rhythms.

But af-ter her lov - er

♩ ♪♪ ♩ ♩ ♩♪♪   S 18-19

♩ | ♪♪ ♩ ♩ ♩ | ♩   A 17-19

♩ ♪♪ ♩ | ♩ ♪   T 18-19

♩ ♪♪ | ♩ ♩ | ♩ ♩   B 18-20

♩ ♩ ♪♪ | ♩ ♩   S 20-21 A 20-21

♩ ♩ ♪♪ | ♪♪   T 21-22 B 21-22

The final example shows a section which is treated with thirteen different rhythms in sixteen appearances. Some of these rhythms are identical in note-value but begin at different places in the measure. These are indicated by brackets.

Up and down   he   wan - - der'd

Rhythm	Voice	Measures	Voice	Measures
	B	23-25		
	T	27-28		
	A	26-28		
	T	23-24		
	S	24-25	T	25-26
	S	26-27	A	25-26
	A	30-32		
	S	31-33		
	S	30-31		
	T	32-33		
	T	31		
	S	28-29	T	29-30
	A	28-30		

Study all of these rhythms. Tap them out with your finger or a pencil. Sing them on a monotone with a neutral syllable, beating time with finger or toe. Sing them on a monotone with the words, going down the list from top to bottom, singing every rhythm correctly.

Stress the long tones no matter what position they occupy in the bar. Make a great distinction between the accented and unaccented notes. Detest characterless singing with no rhythmic high lights or low lights. Despise rhythmic monotony in a piece of this kind. It is better to exaggerate the contrast between accented and unaccented tones than to ignore their rhythmic distinction.

When the singer can sing each of these rhythms with the words in a way to bring out its rhythmic shape or contour, he has the first lesson in how to sing his part in this madrigal.

In a few places the piano version is slightly different from the voice parts. Sometimes the bass is written an octave lower for the piano than for the voice. In such cases all or a few of the basses can sing the part written on the piano staff, if their voices can produce these low tones easily with resonance and volume. Attention is called to these points in measures 6, 12, 18, 19, 20, 33, 43, 47, 57, 67 and 71.

This madrigal opens with a four-measure phrase for the sopranos, which requires great simplicity. It should breathe childlike frankness. It is a simple declaration with no emotional content. An attempt to give it dramatic expression would destroy its simple, naïve beauty. There can be no *tremolo* in any of the voices. The unison must be perfect. Sing rather softly with smooth *legato* and very little accent so this statement will sound as though it were coming from the far distant past, like a story-teller who closes his eyes and begins, "Once upon a time, in the long ago."

When the whole chorus joins in measure 5, there can be a warm, full tone. In measure 7, the sopranos will sing the "eed" very clearly just before the third beat. All other voices sustain the chord on *ah* until the end of the measure. But at the end of the measure, there must be nothing to obscure the word "fair" in the soprano part. Consequently, all other voices will slight the "eed," closing the chord on *ah*. The same thing holds true in measure 13.

The sopranos and chorus then repeat what they have sung, almost as an echo.

Sopranos give firm accents to the syllables "the" and "shep" on the fourth beat of measure 13, and the first beat of measure 14, immediately subordinating the tone to permit the altos to make a prominent entry in measure 14. Each voice as it enters on this phrase must imitate the soprano by accenting the first two tones.

The same holds true in measure 17. The alto starts a new phrase on the fourth beat. This tone is strongly accented with immediate subordination after this one tone as the voices enter only one beat apart. Each voice begins with this one accented tone, but the bass is the only voice which can continue to sing the whole phrase boldly.

In measure 20, the sopranos and altos sing rather daintily. The male voices reply in a more robust manner in measure 21, and measure 22 is very bold and strong. From measure 23 to 28, there is a gradual increase with vigorous and sustained statements in measures 28 and 29.

From the middle of measure 25 to the beginning of measure 33, the bass tone must roll out continuously with no break for breath. Obviously, amateur singers cannot be expected to sing these eight measures with full resonant tone on one breath. If there are eight basses, let the basses breathe in pairs. Each pair will breathe every eight beats, but as there are four pairs, let them breathe two beats apart. This shift should be made on the second and fourth beats so that everyone sings while crossing the bar. Larger or smaller bass sections can be organized according to their sizes. Let as few as possible breathe at one time, but permit each singer to breathe often enough to avoid strain. Each singer will taper his tone off before taking a breath and enter gradually after he has breathed. The mouth should be kept open during breathing, in this case, so the audience cannot see when the breath is taken.

The scale passage for the bass, measures 35-37, is a rich place for the basses. Each of these tones must be attacked with a slight *sforzando*. Although the tone is not large, it must be full of suppressed enthusiasm. "Then they fell a-singing," will be sung with joy in a spirit of exhilaration.

The latter part of the piece is a repetition of measures 24-48 and snould be sung in the same style the second time as the first.

This is the type of piece which can be a terrible bore when sung listlessly. But when sung with enthusiasm and attention to its cross rhythms, it is one of the jolliest and most delightful pieces of its kind.

FAIR PHYLLIS
Madrigal for Mixed Voices

Edited by E. H. Wilcox

JOHN FARMER (fl. 1591-1601)

*) This madrigal may be sung in F#, or F (the original key), if the high tones in any voice prove difficult.

The low G's in the bass part have been written an octave higher. The original is given in the piano part.

45

then they fell a — sing — ing.
theh — (n)thay — (ee)feh — (l)uh — sih — (ng)ih — (ng)

then they fell a sing — — ing.
theh — (n)thay — (ee)feh — (l)uh — sih — — (ng)ih — — (ng)

then they fell a sing-ing. Up and down he
theh — (n)thay — (ee)feh — (l)uh — sih-(ng)ih-(ng)uh-(p)ah-(nd)dah — (oon)hee

then they fell a sing — — ing. Up and
theh — (n)thay — (ee)feh — (l)uh — sih — — (ng)ih — (ng)uh-(p)ah-(nd

50

Up and down he wan-der'd, Up and down he
uh(p)ah-(nd)dah-(oon)hee waw-(n)duh — (rd) uh(p)ah(nd)dah — (oon)hee

Up and down, Up and down he wan-der'd, Up and
uh(p)ah(nd)dah — (oon) uh(p)ah(nd)dah — (oon)hee waw(n)duh — (rd) uh(p)ah(nd

wan — der'd, Up and down, Up and down he wan-der'd,
waw — (n)duh(rd)uh(p)ah-(nd)dah — (oon) uh(p)ah-(nd)dah — (oon)hee waw(n)duh — (rd)

down he wan — — der'd, he wan — —
dah-(oon)hee waw — — (n)duh — (rd)hee waw — — (n)

77384-117

f
wan - der'd, Up and down he wan - der'd,
waw - (n)duh - (rd) uh - (p) ah - (nd) dah - (oon) hee waw - (n)duh - (rd)
f
down he wan - der'd, Up and down he
dah - (oon) hee waw - (n)duh - (rd) uh - (p) ah - (nd) dah - (oon) hee
f
Up and down he wan - der'd, Up and
uh-(p) ah-(nd) dah-(oon) hee waw - (n)duh - (rd) uh - (p) ah - (nd)
f
der'd, Up and
duh - - - (rd) uh - - (p) ah - - - (nd)
f
55
Up and down he wan - der'd, Up and down
uh-(p) ah-(nd) dah-(oon) hee waw - (n)duh - (rd) uh - (p) ah - (nd) dah - (oon)
wan - der'd, Up and down he wan - -
waw - (n)duh - (rd) uh - (p) ah - (nd) dah - (oon) hee waw - - (n)
down he wan - der'd, Up and down he wan - der'd,
dah - (oon) hee waw - (n)duh - (rd) uh-(p) ah-(nd) dah-(oon) hee waw-(n)duh-(rd)
down he
dah - - (oon) hee

f
65
Oh then they fell a - sing - ing, a -
oh theh - (n)thay - (ee)feh - (l)uh - sih - (ng)ih - (ng)uh -
fell a - sing - ing, Oh then they fell a - sing - ing, a -
feh - (l)uh - sih - (ng)ih - (ng) oh theh - (n)thay - (ee)feh - (l)uh - sih - (ng)ih - (ng)uh -
fell a - sing - ing, Oh then they fell a - sing - ing, a -
feh - (l)uh - sih - (ng)ih - (ng) oh theh - (n)thay - (ee)feh - (l)uh - sih - (ng)ih - (ng)uh -
fell a - sing - ing, Oh then they fell a - sing - ing, a -
feh - (l)uh - sih - (ng)ih - (ng) oh theh - (n)thay - (ee)feh - (l)uh - sih - (ng)ih - (ng)uh -
70
ff
sing - ing, Oh then they fell a - sing - ing.
sih - (ng)ih - (ng) oh theh - (n)thay - (ee)feh - (l)uh - sih - (ng)ih - (ng)
sing - ing, Oh then they fell a - sing - ing.
sih - (ng)ih - (ng) oh theh - (n)thay - (ee)feh - (l)uh - sih - (ng)ih - (ng)
sing - ing, Oh then they fell a - sing - ing.
sih - (ng)ih - (ng) oh theh - (n)thay - (ee)feh - (l)uh - sih - (ng)ih - (ng)
sing - ing, Oh then they fell a - sing - ing.
sih - (ng)ih - (ng) oh theh - (n)thay - (ee)feh - (l)uh - sih - (ng)ih - (ng)

Chapter XXIII

SOFT SINGING

As Incense Rises—Dimitri Bortniansky (1752-1825)

Every singer must practice all gradations of sound from *pp* to *ff*, but it is better to err by singing too softly than by swinging to the other extreme and singing too loud. At least, soft singing cannot injure the throat.

The only danger of soft singing comes from permitting a lifeless, devitalized, flabby, uninteresting tone. If the singer can keep his soft tones concentrated, alive, bright and attractive, he will reap rich benefits from soft singing.

Soft singing promotes ease of tone production, flexibility, smoothness, cleanness of enunciation, and tone quality.

As Incense Rises is essentially a soft piece. Although the music rises to *f* at times, it never reaches *ff* and most of the time it is between *pp* and *mp*.

In form it consists of a constantly recurring refrain, sung by the whole chorus, separated by verses for the men's voices alone or the women's voices alone.

In the third measure, the tenors are called upon to sing the high G. If this is difficult, use a combination made of a few altos to double the tenor part, beginning with the last eighth-note in the second measure. The entire alto section may be used for this if necessary.

The tenor sings the same part in measures 9-10 that was assigned to the baritone in measures 7-8, the baritone singing the part previously assigned to the tenor, but one octave lower.

Notice the characteristic rhythm accompanying the cadential chord progression in measures 5-6. The same pattern is used in a quickened form in measures 8, 10 and 12. This rhythmic figure is used many times throughout the composition.

All of the men's voices must be sustained, smooth, firm and strong in measures 15 to 18. Bring the verse to a strong close on the final chord without any *diminuendo*.

When the chorus enters on measure 19, the tone must be very soft, but concentrated and thrilling.

Observe the expression marks minutely because this refrain must be sung with identical expression every time it appears.

There is a principle called "artistic restraint" in the correct interpretation of music. Sometimes this is referred to as "artistic poise." One of its chief elements is the avoidance of exaggeration

164

in interpretation. Exaggeration is one of the most heinous evils in music. When the music is dramatic, the singer must delineate the expression in bold terms and strong contrasts, abandoning himself to the complete expression of great emotion, but there are many times when the artist does not shout his feelings from the housetops.

Often times the things left unsaid are more expressive than what is spoken. Sometimes it is better to give only slight expression to feeling if by so doing one can give an indication of feeling which is held back.

So, in this refrain, there must be a sense of great feeling, but it is suppressed and held back within the heart of the singer who gives only a glimpse of his heart and does not bare his deepest feelings to the public gaze in a melodramatic manner.

The numerous accents on soft dark chords, and the inexorable advance of the rhythm, tend to give the sense of great power in the background.

Beginning at B, the bass will have an urge to forge ahead. He must sing with dignity and dark resonance, but the tone must never become loud. The upper voices should also be restrained. For four measures beginning at C, the deeper bass voices may sing an octave lower, as indicated by the small notes.

This whole refrain is restrained, dark in color, and sung in the softer gradations of tone volume.

The ensuing trio for women's voices has somewhat brighter tone quality, the final five measures starting with a rather loud swell which decreases to a soft final chord. The first syllable of the word "Father" is spelled phonetically as "fah." Avoid a thin tone. In some places this syllable is sung almost "faw" to insure a solid resonant tone of dark tone color. The correct sound is midway between the two spellings, leaning toward one or the other, depending on whether a dark or bright quality is desired. In this case we lean toward the brighter side. At the end of the last piece in this book, is a striking example of the use of the dark quality on this word.

After the return of the refrain, the men's voices sing alone again. This requires vigorous, rather masculine singing, especially after the first four measures where the tenor begins with the positive half-notes. From that point on, the male voices sing with a decidedly masculine and virile tone quality and style. Expression marks are given in complete detail for the final women's trio and the return to the men's chorus.

This whole number discloses a religious experience which consists of a deep worship within the heart rather than striking outward demonstrations.

AS INCENSE RISES

For Mixed Voices

Translated by *E. H. Wilcox*

DIMITRI BORTNIANSKY (1752-182
Edited by E. H. Wilcox

77384-1

Mixed Voices
SOPRANO
ALTO
TENOR
BASS
A
May my plea a-rise on wings to the skies,
may-(ee)mah-(ee)plee uh-rah-(eez)aw-(n)wih-(ngz)too thuh skah-(eez)
B
As in-cense ris-es from the al-tar. May I
ah-(z)ih-(n)seh-(ns)rah-(eez)eh-(z) fraw-(m)thee aw-(l)tuh-(r) may-(ee)ah-(ee)

p 45 mp
hear my plea. I raise my voice, O Fa -
hee - (r)mah - (ee)plee ah - (ee)ray - (eez)mah - (ee)vaw(ees) oh fah -
p 45 mp
hear my plea. I raise my voice, O
hee - (r)mah - (ee)plee ah - (ee)ray - - (eez)mah - (ee)vaw - (ees) oh
p 45 mp
hear my plea. I raise my voice, O
hee - (r)mah - (ee)plee ah - (ee)ray - (eez)mah - (ee)vaw - (ees) oh
45 p mp
mf
- ther com - pas - sion - ate, I cry to
thuh - (r)kaw - (m)pah - shuh - (n)eh - (t) ah - (ee)krah - (ee)too
mf
Fa - ther com - pas - sion - ate, I cry to
fah - thuh - (r)kaw - (m)pah - shuh - (n)eh - (t) ah - (ee)krah - (ee)too
mf
Fa - ther com - pas - sion - ate, I
fah - thuh - (r)kaw - (m)pah - shuh - (n)eh - (t) ah - (ee)
mf
50 p
Thee, O lov - ing God.
thee oh luh - (v)ih - (ng)gaw - (d)
50 p
Thee, O lov - ing God.
thee oh luh - (v)ih - (ng)gaw - (d)
50 p
cry to Thee, O lov - ing God.
krah - (ee)too thee oh luh - (v)ih - (ng)gaw - (d)
50 p

Mixed Voices

Mixed Voices

SOPRANO

pp

A

May my plea a – rise on wings to the skies,

may - (ee) mah - (ee) plee uh – rah-(eez) aw – (n) wih – (ngz) too thuh skah - (eez)

ALTO

pp

May my plea a – rise on wings to the skies,

may - (ee) mah - (ee) plee uh – rah-(eez) aw – (n) wih – (ngz) too thuh skah - (eez)

TENOR

pp

May my plea a – rise on wings to the skies,

may - (ee) mah - (ee) plee uh – rah-(eez) aw – (n) wih – (ngz) too thuh skah - (eez)

BASS

pp

May my plea a – rise on wings to the skies,

may - (ee) mah - (ee) plee uh – rah-(eez) aw – (n) wih – (ngz) too thuh skah - (eez)

A

pp

p *pp* B *p*

As in – cense ris – es from the al – tar. May I

ah-(z) ih-(n) seh-(ns) rah-(eez) eh-(z) fraw-(m) thee aw-(l) tuh-(r) may - (ee) ah-(ee)

p *pp* *p*

As in – cense ris – es from the al – tar. May I

ah-(z) ih-(n) seh-(ns) rah-(eez) eh-(z) fraw-(m) thee aw-(l) tuh-(r) may - (ee) ah-(ee)

p *pp* *p*

As in – cense ris – es from the al – tar. May I

ah – (z) ih-(n) seh-(ns) rah-(eez) eh-(z) fraw – (m) thee aw-(l) tuh-(r) may - (ee) ah-(ee

p *pp* *p*

As in – cense ris – es from the al – tar. May I

ah-(z) ih-(n) seh-(ns) rah-(eez) eh-(z) fraw-(m) thee aw-(l) tuh-(r) may - (ee) ah-(ee)

B

p *pp* *p*

please my God. My arms are lift- ed in eve-ning
plee-(z)mah-(ee)gaw - (d)mah-(ee)ah - (rmz)ah - (r)lih - (f)teh-(d) ih - (n)ee-(v)nih(ng)

please my God. My arms are lift- ed in eve-ning
plee-(z)mah-(ee)gaw - (d)mah-(ee)ah - (rmz)ah - (r)lih - (f)teh-(d) ih - (n)ee-(v)nih(ng)

please my God. My arms are lift- ed in eve-ning
plee - (z)mah- (ee) gaw-(d)mah-(ee)ah - (rmz)ah - (r)lih - (f)teh-(d) ih - (n)ee-(v)nih(ng)

please___ my God. My___ arms are lift- ed in eve-ning
plee - (z)mah- (ee)gaw-(d) mah - (ee)zh(rmz)ah - (r)lih - (f)teh-(d) ih - (n)ee-(v)nih(ng)

sac - ri - fice, in eve - ning sac - ri - fice.
sah - (k)rih - fah - (ees)ih - (n)ee - (v)nih - (ng)sah - (k)rih - fah - (ees)

sac - ri - fice, in eve - ning sac - ri - fice.
sah - (k)rih - fah - (ees)ih - (n)ee - (v)nih - (ng)sah - (k)rih - fah - (ees)

sac - ri - fice, in eve - ning sac - ri - fice.
sah - (k)rih - fah - (ees)ih - (n)ee - (v)nih - (ng)sah - (k)rih - fah - (ees)

sac - ri - fice, in eve - ning sac - ri - fice.
sah - (k)rih - fah - (ees)ih - (n)ee - (v)nih - (ng)sah - (k)rih - fah - (ees)

77384-117

115
let me con - done my own sin, Do not
leh - (t)mee kah - (n)doh - (n)mah - (ee)oh - (n)sih - (n) doo naw - (t)
let me con - done my own sin, Do not
leh - (t)mee kah - (n)doh - (n)mah - (ee)oh - (n)sih - (n) doo naw - (t)
let me con - done my own sin, Do not
leh - (t)mee kah - (n)doh - (n)mah - (ee)oh - (n)sih - (n) doo naw - (t)
let me con - done my own sin. O
leh - (t)mee kah - (n)doh - (n) mah - (ee)oh - (n)sih - (n) oh
let me con - done my own sin. O
leh - (t)mee kah - (n)doh - (n) mah - (ee)oh - (n)sih - (n) oh
let me con - done my own sin. O
leh - (t)mee kah - (n)doh - (n) mah - (ee)oh - (n)sih - (n) oh
rall.
120
Lento
Fa - ther, O Fa - ther, hear my plea.
fah - thuh - (r) oh fah - thuh - (r) hee - (r)mah - (ee)plee
Fa - ther, O Fa - ther, hear my plea.
fah - thuh - (r) oh fah - thuh - (r) hee - (r)mah - (ee)plee
Fa - ther, O Fa - ther, hear my plea.
fah - thuh - (r) oh fah - thuh - (r) hee - (r)mah - (ee)plee

Mixed voices
SOPRANO
pp
p
135
May I please my God. My arms are lift - ed
may - (ee) ah-(ee)plee-(z)mah-(ee)gaw - (d)mah-(ee)ah - (rmz) ah-(r)lih - (f)teh-(d)
ALTO
May I please my God. My arms are lift - ed
may - (ee) ah-(ee)plee-(z)mah-(ee)gaw - (d)mah-(ee)ah - (rmz) ah-(r)lih - (f)teh-(d)
TENOR
May I please my God. My arms are lift - ed
may - (ee) ah-(ee)plee - (z)mah-(ee)gaw-(d)mah(ee)ah - (rmz) ah-(r)lih - (f)teh-(d)
BASS
May I please my God. My arms are lift - ed
may - (ee) ah-(ee)plee - (z)mah-(ee)gaw-(d)mah - (ee) ah-(rmz)ah-(r)lih - (f)teh-(d)
mp
pp
in eve-ning sac-ri-fice, in eve-ning sac - ri - fice.
ih - (n)ee-(v)nih-(ng)sah-(k)rih-fah-(ees)ih - (n)ee-(v)nih-(ng)sah - (k)rih - fah - (ees)

Chapter XXIV

DYNAMIC VARIETY

Pater Noster—Peter Ilyitch Tchaikovsky (1840-1893)

THIS book calls for six gradations of volume in its musical illustrations. Three of these are on the loud side and three are on the soft side. Starting from the median point and decreasing the volume, we pass through *mp–p–pp*. Beginning at the same point and increasing the volume, we have *mf–f–ff*. These relationships are illustrated in a long swell, starting from *pp*, moving to *ff*, and returning to *pp*.

pp - p - mp - mf - f - ff - f - mf - mp - p - pp

Although this looks simple, it is exceedingly difficult to pass through the six degrees of tone volume several times and give the same value to each gradation each time.

It is a profitable exercise for each singer to practice a neutral syllable on a monotone, singing it

mf --- f --- ff --- f --- mf

The problem here is to sing *ff* without sacrificing quality. Avoid a raucous quality on the loudest tones. Sing them as easily as possible. Keep the tone free and unimpeded. Do not strain the vocal mechanism. Listen intently to vowel quality which must not change as the volume of tone is altered.

After he is sure of these three gradations, he should start one degree softer, using the same monotone and neutral syllable to move toward the soft side.

mp --- p --- pp --- p --- mp

The difficulty here is to keep the tone pointed, energetic, vital and spinning although it is soft. Avoid a flabby, mushy, muffled or devitalized tone. The perfect *pp* will have a concentrated, spinning quality which gives great carrying power, and makes a tone sound almost as loud in the farthest balcony as it sounds on the stage.

Now it will be possible to put the two exercises together as follows:

pp-p-mp-mf-f-ff-f-mf-mp-p - pp-p-mp-mf-f-ff-f-mf-mp-p-pp

Each singer will practice the exercises in Chapter III at each of the six degrees of volume. Also give additional study to the swell exercise in Chapter VI.

After the individual singer has studied these gradations, the chorus as a whole should sing them. Also rehearse individual tones and chords, repeating them through all of the six degrees of volume, always returning to the starting point. Sometimes detach these chords and at other times produce them in the form of a smooth swell.

Pater Noster gives every opportunity to study these six gradations of tone. Starting *pp*, it begins measure 5 *mp*, returns to *p* in measure 8 and attains *f* in measure 13. After noting the relation between *p* and *mf* in measures 15 and 17, there is a brilliant *f* in measures 23-24 and a glorious *ff* in measures 33-34.

The entire composition is filled with contrasting measures, utilizing every gradation of volume and many types of articulation from smooth *legato* to *staccato*, strong accent, and *sforzando*.

This lovely movement should be sung with dignity, reverence and deep feeling. Complete expression marks have been added.

Start the first chord softly but with the carefully balanced parts. The tenor is most important. He is the first to begin the swell. The first tone of the second measure will be accented in the tenor part to emphasize the skip.

The notes with a straight horizontal line above them must be slightly detached but pressed firmly with the breath to give them nearly their full value and to make them prominent.

Other parts must subordinate to the tenor in measures 7-8. The bass in measures 9-10 imitates the tenor of measures 7-8 an octave lower. This imitation must be obvious to the listener. The bass will be prominent in measures 9-10.

In measures 5-6 and the first beat of measure 7, the alto and tenor parts are changed from the original edition in deference to choruses in which the tenors do not sing the high *G* easily. A chorus which has tenors who can sing these high tones, should trade parts between altos and tenors, thereby returning to the parts originally intended by the composer. If there are only one or two tenors who can sing these tones, even lightly, let them sing with the altos on this part in order to give it body.

Hold the chord without *diminuendo* through measures 13-14.

At measure 15, the tone color is extremely dark, but at measure 23, it becomes very bright.

Beginning with measure 27, there is a scale passage covering two octaves and one step in four measures with the help of each voice part. It begins in the bass moving upward by quarter-notes from *D* to *A* in measure 27. On the tone *A* the tenors carry the scale on up to *E* where it is taken by the altos to *A*. The sopranos carry the scale on up to *E*. The voice parts must blend with each other where the scale passes from one section to another in order to avoid any unevenness in the steady progress of the scale. Each tone of this entire scale must be pressed with the breath but slightly detached from its neighbor in order to give it prominence.

Take plenty of time for breath before starting measure 31.

Make an abrupt release at the end of the chord in measure 34. This is followed by a long pause. Do not hurry to start the following measure. Be very deliberate on this rest.

Starting at measure 35, there is a beautiful fugal passage with each voice answering its predecessor. The composer wrote the first statement of this subject in measures 35-36 for tenors alone. Sing it that way in every case where the tenors can produce the top *G* easily. But if the tenors find the top tones difficult, add altos as indicated in the music. Use only the number of altos necessary to strengthen the tenors. The entire alto section will not be needed unless there are few or no tenors to sing this part. Any tenor singer who cannot sing the top *G* easily, should rest in measures 35-36, letting the altos take his place. Beginning with measure 37, all tenors will be able to sing their part.

If the altos have not sung in measures 35-36, they will sing measures 37-38 without the aid of any sopranos. But if the altos have been helping the tenors, a few sopranos must help the altos in measures 37-38 in order to produce a new tone quality and give prominence to the subject in measures 37-38. Most of the sopranos will be saved for their entrance in measure 39 where the sopranos all combine to sing their own solo. The bass solo at measure 41 must be full of dignity and nobility.

Observe the bass accents in measure 44. These tones are detached to give a mysterious effect almost like the *pizzicato* of the orchestral string bass.

Detach the chords in measures 47-48 and sing *legato* as a contrast in measures 50-51-52. The tone becomes extremely sombre in measures 53-54-55. Detach the chords again in measure 56 and make a contrast by *legato* singing immediately thereafter. The final detached treatment occurs in measure 63, followed by the *legato* contrast.

The final three measures are sung brightly, with the original tempo, and without *diminuendo* on the final chord.

PATER NOSTER

For Mixed Voices

Edited by John Smallman

PETER ILYITCH TCHAIKOVSKY (1840-1893)

77384-117

in coe - lis: Sanc - ti - fi - ce - tur no - men
- (s)ee - (n)chay - lee - (s) sah-(nk)tee - fee - kay - too - (r)noh - meh-(n)
in coe - lis: Sanc - ti - fi - ce - tur no - men
- (s)ee - (n)chay - lee - (s) sah-(nk)tee - fee - kay - too - (r)noh - meh-(n)
- - lis: Sanc - ti - fi - ce - tur no - men
- - lee - - (s) sah-(nk)tee - fee - kay - too - (r)noh - meh-(n)
in coe - lis: Sanc - ti - fi - ce - tur no - men
ee - (n)chay - lee - (s) sah-(nk)tee - fee - kay - too - (r)noh - meh-(n)
tu - um: Ad - ve - ni - at re - gnum tu - um: Fi -
too - oo - (m) ah - (d)vay - nee - ah - (t)ray - (n)yoo - (m)too - oo - (m) fee -
tu - um: Ad - ve - ni - at re - gnum tu - um: Fi -
too - oo - (m) ah - (d)vay - nee - ah - (t)ray - (n)yoo - (m)too - oo - (m) fee -
tu - um: Ad - ve - ni - at re - gnum tu - um:
too - oo - (m) ah - (d)vay - nee - ah - (t)ray - (n)yoo - (m)too - oo - (m)
tu - um. Ad - ve - ni - at re - gnum tu - um: Fi -
too - oo - (m) ah - (d)vay - nee - ah - (t)ray - (n)yoo - (m)too - oo - (m) fee -

at vo - lun - tas tu - a, si - cut
ah - (t)voh - loo - (n)tah - (s)too - ah see - koo -
at vo - lun - tas tu - a, si - cut
ah - (t)voh - loo - (n)tah - (s)too - ah see - koo - (t)
Fi - at vo - lun - tas tu - a, si - cut
fee - ah - (t)voh - loo - (n)tah - (s)too - ah see - koo - (t)
at vo - lun - tas tu - a, si - cut
ah - (t)voh - loo - (n)tah - (s)too - ah see - koo - (t)
in coe - lo, et in ter - ra.
- (t)ee - (n)chay - loh eh - (t)ee - (n)teh - rah
in coe - lo, et in ter - ra.
ee - (n)chay - loh eh - (t)ee - (n)teh - rah
in coe - lo, et in ter - ra.
ee - (n)chay - loh eh - (t)ee - (n)teh - rah
in coe - lo, et in ter - ra.
ee - (n)chay - loh eh - (t)ee - (n)teh - rah

* The small notes to be sung only by a few Altos to reenforce Tenors when necessary.

Chapter XXV

SIMPLICITY

Almighty Father—Johann Sebastian Bach (1685-1750)

Bach was one of the most accomplished composers the world has ever known. Some of his compositions have great complexity He was able to write the most intricate type of music, yet many of his greatest pages are simplicity exemplified.

The chorals of Bach, together with his other church music, stand as the highest expression of Protestant music. These chorals seem to breathe the dignified simplicity of the early followers of Luther.

Maintain dignity in the pronunciation of such words as "fulfill." The first syllable is based on a tone midway between *uh* and *oo* although the phonetic spelling is *uh*. Lean toward the *oo* tone enough to produce a dignified, full quality.

This particular choral is extremely simple, but it voices a prayer of great humility and beauty. As stated in a previous chapter, exaggeration of expression is the height of vulgarity. Sing this number frankly and in a straightforward manner. Hold the points of rest without relaxation, and take plenty of time for breath. Think of the text as you sing it. If you can make the text a part of you, the expression will take care of itself.

It is appropriate to mention again a point which was referred to in connection with our first composition. The "straight-line tone" is the ideal tone for choral singing. One voice with a *tremolo* can destroy the blend and intonation of a whole chorus. But occasionally, an immature or inexperienced singer thinks a *tremolo* is dramatic and desirable. A *tremolo* is more than dramatic, it is melodramatic, super-sentimental, amateurish, and sickening. Tenors with a bleat, basses with a wobble, and female voices that throb, pulsate and oscillate are a curse to the ears. The first and last problem of the choral singer is to produce a single sustained tone of beautiful quality which can be maintained in simple purity without variation of any kind from beginning to end. The beginner must strive for this. The experienced artist, after attaining good technical dexterity, will return to the daily routine of practicing sustained tones, trying to produce one tone which will be so simple and unchanging from beginning to end that it gives a hint of perfection

Avoid affectation, cultivate simplicity and sincerity, even in the production of the least important tone. Sing with an even, unwavering, spinning tone, and let that tone be lost in the blend with the other voices on your part. Then will the conductor call down blessings upon your head and name you the child of Orpheus.

ALMIGHTY FATHER

Edited by John Smallman

Melody by
JOHANN CRÜGER (1598-1662)
Harmonized by Johann Sebastian Bach
(1685-1750)

77384-117

p
ca - tion. Hear Thou our pray'r, the spoken and un -
kay - (ee) shuh-(n)hee - (r) thah-(oo)ah - (oor) preh - (r)thuh spoh - keh-(n)ah-(nd)uh - (n)
ca - tion. Hear Thou our pray'r, the spo - ken and un -
ca - tion. Hear Thou our pray'r, the spo - ken and un -
ca - tion. Hear Thou our pray'r, the spo - ken and un -
pp
p allargando
10
spo - ken. Hear us, our Fa - ther.
spoh - keh - (n) hee - (r) uh - (s) ah - (oor) fah - thuh - (r)
spo - ken. Hear us, our Fa - ther
spo - ken. Hear us, our Fa - ther.
spo - ken Hear us, our Fa - ther.
allargando

mp
Al - migh - ty Fa - ther, from Thy watch and
aw - (l)mah - (ee)tee fah - thuh - (r)fraw - (m)thah-(ee)waw - (tch)ah - (nd)
mp
Al - migh - ty Fa - ther, from Thy watch and
aw - (l)mah - (ee)tee fah - thuh - (r)fraw - (m)thah-(ee)waw - (tch)ah - (nd)
mp
Al - migh - ty Fa - ther, from Thy watch and
aw - (l)mah - (ee)tee fah - thuh - (r)fraw - (m)thah-(ee)waw - (tch)ah - (nd)
mp
Al - migh - ty Fa - ther, from Thy watch and
aw - (l)mah - (ee)tee fah - thuh - (r)fraw - (m)thah-(ee)waw - (tch)ah - (nd)
mp
mf
15
f
keep - ing No place can part nor hour of time re -
kee - (p)ih-(ng)noh play-(ees)kah-(n)pah - (rt)noh - (r) ah-(oor)aw - (v)tah-(eem)ree -
keep - ing No place can part nor hour of time re -
kee - (p)ih-(ng)noh play-(ees)kah-(n)pah - (rt)noh - (r) ah-(oor)aw - (v)tah-(eem)ree -
keep - ing No place can part nor hour of time re -
kee - (p)ih-(ng)noh play-(ees)kah-(n)pah - (rt)noh - (r) ah-(oor)aw - (v)tah-(eem)ree -
keep - ing No place can part nor hour of time re -
kee - (p)ih-(ng)noh play-(ees)kah-(n)pah - (rt)noh - (r) ah-(oor)aw - (v)tah-(eem)ree -
15
mf
f

move us. Give us Thy good and save us from all
moo - (v)uh-(s)gih - (v)uh - (s)thah-(ee)goo - (d)ah - (nd)say-(eev)uh-(s)fraw-(m)aw - (l)

e - - vil. Hear us, our Fa - ther.
ee - - (v)ih - (l)hee - (r)uh - (s)ah - (oor)fah - thuh - (r)

pp *p allargando*

allargando